W9-CYW-097

JOURNEYS

Reader's Notebook

Volume 2

Grade 1

HOUGHTON MIFFLIN HARCOURT
School Publishers

Copyright © by Houghton Mifflin Harcourt Publishing Company

All rights reserved. No part of this work may be reproduced or transmitted in any form or by any means, electronic or mechanical, including photocopying or recording, or by any information storage or retrieval system, without the prior written permission of the copyright owner unless such copying is expressly permitted by federal copyright law.

Permission is hereby granted to individuals using the corresponding student's textbook or kit as the major vehicle for regular classroom instruction to photocopy entire pages from this publication in classroom quantities for instructional use and not for resale. Requests for information on other matters regarding duplication of this work should be addressed to Houghton Mifflin Harcourt Publishing Company, Attn: Contracts, Copyrights, and Licensing, 9400 Southpark Center Loop, Orlando, Florida 32819.

Printed in the U.S.A.

ISBN 978-0-547-86061-9

19 20 0982 21 20 19 18 17 16 15

4500535285 B C D E F G

If you have received these materials as examination copies free of charge, Houghton Mifflin Harcourt Publishing Company retains title to the materials and they may not be resold. Resale of examination copies is strictly prohibited.

Possession of this publication in print format does not entitle users to convert this publication, or any portion of it, into electronic format.

Contents

Unit 4

Lesson 16:	Let's Go to the Moon!	1
Lesson 17:	The Big Trip	16
Lesson 18:	Where Does Food Come From?	31
Lesson 19:	Tomás Rivera	46
Lesson 20:	Little Rabbit's Tale	62

Unit 5

Lesson 21:	The Garden	78
Lesson 22:	Amazing Animals	93
Lesson 23:	Whistle for Willie	108
Lesson 24:	A Tree Is a Plant	123
Lesson 25:	The New Friend	138

Unit 6

Lesson 26:	The Dot	152
Lesson 27:	What Can You Do?	167
Lesson 28:	The Kite	182
Lesson 29:	Hi! Fly Guy	197
Lesson 30:	Winners Never Quit!	212

© Houghton Mifflin Harcourt Publishing Company. All rights reserved.

Name _____

Let's Go to the Moon!
Phonics: Words with Long *o*

Words with Long *o*

Read the word. Circle the picture that matches the word.

1.

home

2.

go

3.

stone

4.

robe

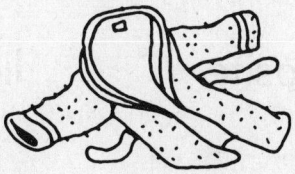

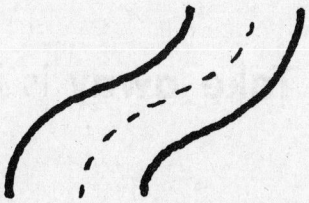

5.

hole

© Houghton Mifflin Harcourt Publishing Company. All rights reserved.

Name _____

Words to Know

Listen to the clues and read along.
Circle the best answer to each clue.

1. This means **in a circle.**	**around**	**think**
2. This means **not heavy.**	**because**	**light**
3. You do this to let people look at something.	**bring**	**show**
4. After is its opposite.	**before**	**carry**
5. You do this with bags.	**carry**	**because**
6. This tells why.	**because**	**around**
7. Take away is its opposite.	**light**	**bring**
8. Your brain does this.	**think**	**before**

© Houghton Mifflin Harcourt Publishing Company. All rights reserved.

Name _____

Let's Go to the Moon!
Phonics: Words with Long *o*

Words with Long *o*

Look at the picture. Name each picture.
Write the missing letters to complete the word.

1.

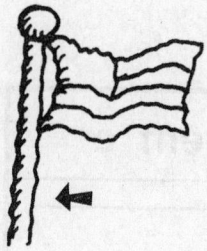

p ___ l ___

2.

b ___ n ___

3.

g ___

4.

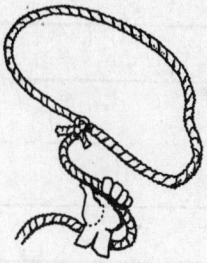

r ___ p ___

5.

s t ___ v ___

6.

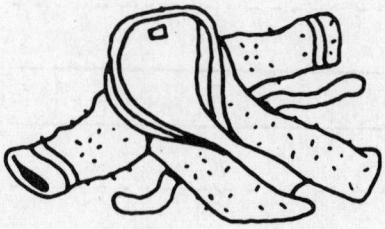

r ___ b ___

© Houghton Mifflin Harcourt Publishing Company. All rights reserved.

Name _____

Let's Go to the Moon!
Spelling: Words with Long *o*

Spelling Words with the Long *o* Sound

Sort the words. Write the correct Spelling Words in each column.

Ends with o	Ends with Silent e

Spelling Words

so
go
home
hole
no
rope
joke
bone
stove
poke

© Houghton Mifflin Harcourt Publishing Company. All rights reserved.

Name _____

What Is a Question?

Circle each question.

1. What did you see?

2. Can you look up?

3. Is that the sun?

4. I think I will read.

5. Where did Mike go?

6. They are at the game.

7. How many rocks does Liz have?

8. I like to tell jokes.

Choose one question. Add details.

_____

_____

_____

_____

© Houghton Mifflin Harcourt Publishing Company. All rights reserved.

Name _____

Let's Go to the Moon!
Writing: Narrative Writing

Using Details

Draw a picture of something you discovered, or found.

Write sentences about when you saw your discovery.

One day I **found** a _____ _____.

When I **saw** it, I _____ _____.

Then I _____.

Main Idea

All my sentences tell about _____.

© Houghton Mifflin Harcourt Publishing Company. All rights reserved.

Name _____

Let's Go to the Moon!
Phonics: Words with Long *u*

Words with Long *u*

Circle the word that names the picture.

1.

flute flat

2.

mole mule

3.

hang huge

4.

cute cut

5.

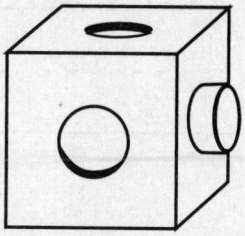

cone cube

© Houghton Mifflin Harcourt Publishing Company. All rights reserved.

Name _____ Date _____

Reader's Guide

Let's Go to the Moon!

Interview an Astronaut

Today you are a reporter. A reporter asks a person questions and writes down the answers. Read pages 20–23. Think about what you read. Then write a question you would like to ask an astronaut. Then pretend to be the astronaut. Write the answer.

Q: _____

A: _____

© Houghton Mifflin Harcourt Publishing Company. All rights reserved.

Name _____ Date _____

Let's Go to the Moon!
Independent Reading

Read pages 28–33. Think about what you read. Write a question you would like to ask an astronaut. Then pretend to be the astronaut. Write your answer.

Q:

A:

© Houghton Mifflin Harcourt Publishing Company. All rights reserved.

Name _____

Let's Go to the Moon!
Spelling: Words with Long *o*

Spelling Words with the Long *o* Sound

Spelling Words

so
go
home
hole
no
rope
joke
bone
stove
poke

Write the Spelling Words that rhyme with **woke**.

1. _____ 2. _____

Write the Spelling Words that begin with **h**.

3. _____ 4. _____

Write the Spelling Words that rhyme with **Jo**.

5. _____

6. _____

7. _____

© Houghton Mifflin Harcourt Publishing Company. All rights reserved.

Name _____

Writing Questions

Write the correct word from the Word Bank to begin each sentence. Write the correct end mark.

Word Bank

What Can When Where Do Are

1. _____ can I put my hat _____

2. _____ can they see _____

3. _____ you see me _____

4. _____ you need a snack _____

5. _____ you cold _____

6. _____ do you go _____

© Houghton Mifflin Harcourt Publishing Company. All rights reserved.

Name _____

Planning My Sentences

Let's Go to the Moon!
Writing: Narrative Writing

Draw and write details that tell what happened.

My Topic: _____

First Detail

Second Detail

Last Detail

© Houghton Mifflin Harcourt Publishing Company. All rights reserved.

Name _____

Let's Go to the Moon!
Spelling: Words with Long *o*

Spelling Words with the Long *o* Sound

Write a Spelling Word to complete each sentence.

Spelling Words

so
go
home
hole
no
rope
joke
bone
stove
poke

1. The pot on the _____ is hot.

2. Can you wrap the _____ around the pole?

3. What _____ does a fox live in?

4. I can tell a funny _____.

5. Stand up _____ that I can see you.

6. It is time to _____ to bed.

© Houghton Mifflin Harcourt Publishing Company. All rights reserved.

Name _____

Spiral Review

Circle each proper noun. Some of them have two words in their name. Then write the proper noun correctly.

1. My friend mel has a box of gem stones. Mel

2. We live in oak lane. oak lane

3. She has a cat named red. red

4. I saw the dog show. dog

Draw a line under each title. Then write the titles and names correctly.

5. Mom's friend is mrs. Dell. Mrs Dell

6. Will dr. Wade visit the class? Dr Wade

© Houghton Mifflin Harcourt Publishing Company. All rights reserved.

Name _____

Grammar in Writing

Let's Go to the Moon!
Grammar: Questions

A sentence that asks something is called a **question.** A question begins with a capital letter and ends with a **question mark.**

Fix the mistakes in these sentences. Use proofreading marks.

Examples: does the moon have plants
Is the moon dusty.

1. Did you know his name
2. when did they go?
3. Why do you have your bike.
4. what do cats eat?
5. is the Moon hot or cold.

Proofreading Marks	
^	Add
≡	Capital letter

© Houghton Mifflin Harcourt Publishing Company. All rights reserved.

Name _____

The Big Trip
Phonics: Words with Long *e*

Words with Long *e*

Circle the word that matches the picture.

1.

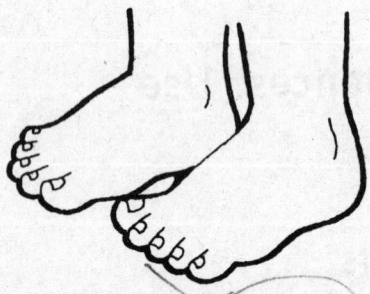

feel feet

2.

tree tea

3.

me he

4.

leaf leap

5.

seat street

6.

see bee

© Houghton Mifflin Harcourt Publishing Company. All rights reserved.

Name _____

The Big Trip
High-Frequency Words

Words to Know

Listen to the questions. Read along. Circle the best answer to each question.

1. What word goes with **might**? maybe there
2. What word goes with **do not**? car don't
3. What word goes with **true**? could sure
4. What word goes with **drive**? car there
5. What word goes with **here**? there don't
6. What word goes with **can**? cart could
7. What word comes after the words "**This story is** _____"? don't about
8. What word tells how you travel? by maybe

© Houghton Mifflin Harcourt Publishing Company. All rights reserved.

Name _____

The Big Trip
Phonics: Words with Long *e*

Words with Long *e*

Circle the word that completes the sentence.

1. I can _____ you how to plant seeds.

teach **beach**

2. These are big _____.

bees **seeds**

3. I will put them in _____ holes.

jeep **deep**

4. Help me _____ my watering can.

reach **peach**

5. Before long, we will see a small _____.

beef **leaf**

© Houghton Mifflin Harcourt Publishing Company. All rights reserved.

The Big Trip
Spelling: Words with Long *e*

Name _____

Spelling Words with the Long *e* Sound

Sort the words. Write the correct Spelling Words in each column.

Words with e	Words with ea	Words with ee

Word with Silent e

Spelling Words

me
be
read
feet
tree
keep
eat
mean
sea
these

© Houghton Mifflin Harcourt Publishing Company. All rights reserved.

Name _____

The Big Trip
Grammar: Compound Sentences

Compound Sentences

Draw a line under the correct compound sentence in each pair.

1. Max took the bus, and we walked.

Max took the bus and we walked.

2. Do you know, or should I tell you.

Do you know, or should I tell you?

3. Work quickly, but be careful.

Work quickly, but be careful?

Write the correct end mark to finish each compound sentence.

4. Stay in line, and wait for the bell ____

5. Is your sister here, or is she at home ____

© Houghton Mifflin Harcourt Publishing Company. All rights reserved.

Name _____

The Big Trip
Writing: Narrative Writing

Details for Where and When

Draw a picture of something you saw or did on a trip.

Write sentences about your trip.

Who	Action	Where

Who	Action	When

Who	Action	Where

© Houghton Mifflin Harcourt Publishing Company. All rights reserved.

Name _____

The Big Trip
Phonics: Words Ending with *ng, nk*

Words Ending with *ng, nk*

Circle the letters that finish the word.

Write the word.

1.

ba____

(nk, ng)

_____

_____

2.

dri____

(nk, ng)

_____

_____

3.

swi____

(nk, ng)

_____

_____

4.

ki____

(nk, ng)

_____

_____

© Houghton Mifflin Harcourt Publishing Company. All rights reserved.

Name _____ Date _____

Reader's Guide

The Big Trip

Travel Riddles

Let's have fun with riddles about **The Big Trip**! Read the clues and the question. Write the answer in a sentence.

I have two wheels. I am pulled by an animal. What am I? ***Do you need a clue? Read pages 60–61.***

_____

_____.

I have no wheels. You can ride in my basket. I go in the air. What am I? ***Do you need a clue? Read pages 64–65.***

_____

_____.

I have four wheels. You can put your suitcase on top of me. What am I? ***Do you need a clue? Read pages 56–57.***

_____

_____.

© Houghton Mifflin Harcourt Publishing Company. All rights reserved.

Name _____ Date _____

The Big Trip
Independent Reading

Now you write a travel riddle! After you write your riddle, share it with a friend. A riddle gives clues. You write the clues. Then a riddle asks a question. The question is already written. You write the answer. Do not let your friend see it! Write the pages from **The Big Trip** where your reader can find clues.

Clues: _____

What kind of travel am I? _____

Do you need a clue? Read pages: _____

© Houghton Mifflin Harcourt Publishing Company. All rights reserved.

Name _____

The Big Trip
Spelling: Words with Long *e*

Spelling Words with the Long *e* Sound

Write the Spelling Word that names each picture.

Spelling Words

me
be
read
feet
tree
keep
eat
mean
sea
these

1. _____

2. _____

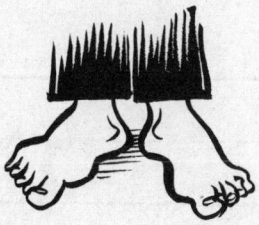

3. _____

4. _____

5. _____

6. _____

© Houghton Mifflin Harcourt Publishing Company. All rights reserved.

Name _____

Writing Compound Sentences

Write a compound sentence by combining each pair of shorter sentences.

1. Are you ready? Should I wait?

or

2. Walk the dog. Feed the cat.

and

3. I feel good. Joe is sick.

but

© Houghton Mifflin Harcourt Publishing Company. All rights reserved.

Name _____

Planning My Sentences

The Big Trip
Writing: Narrative Writing

Draw and write details that tell what happened first, next, and last.

My Topic: _____

First

Next

Last

© Houghton Mifflin Harcourt Publishing Company. All rights reserved.

Name _____

The Big Trip
Spelling: Words with Long *e*

Spelling Words with the Long *e* Sound

Write a Spelling Word from the box to complete each sentence.

Spelling Words

me
be
read
feet
tree
keep
eat
mean
sea
these

1. Look at the leaves on that _____ _____ _____.

2. What do you _____ in your backpack? _____ _____

3. I like to swim in the _____. _____ _____

4. Pick from _____ games. _____ _____

5. A duck has two _____. _____ _____

6. Will you _____ to me?

© Houghton Mifflin Harcourt Publishing Company. All rights reserved.

Name _____

Spiral Review

Draw a line under each command.

1. We watched the game.
2. Watch where you walk.
3. Be kind to the animals.
4. What kind of dog is that?

Add words to each command to make a compound sentence.

5. Wait for your turn.

_____

_____

_____

_____

_____

_____

6. Listen carefully.

_____

_____

_____

_____

_____

_____

© Houghton Mifflin Harcourt Publishing Company. All rights reserved.

Name _____

Grammar in Writing

The Big Trip
Grammar: Compound Sentences

A **compound sentence** is made up of two shorter sentences joined by a comma and **and, but,** or **or.**

Underline each compound sentence.

1. The girls walked or rode the bus to school.

2. Mom drives to work, but Dad takes a train.

3. Is the game today, or is it tomorrow?

Write a compound sentence by combining the two shorter sentences.

4. Take a nap. Don't be late.

but

5. I have paper. Larry has pencils.

and

© Houghton Mifflin Harcourt Publishing Company. All rights reserved.

Name _____

Where Does Food Come From?
Phonics: Words with *ai, ay*

Words with *ai*, *ay*

Read the words. Circle the word that names the picture. Then write the word.

1.

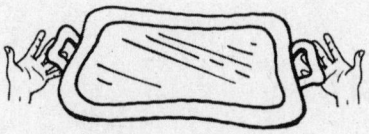

tray ray

_____

2.

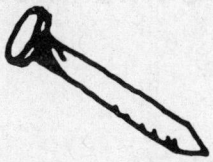

sail nail

_____

3.

hay day

_____

4.

paint pain

_____

5.

train rain

_____

© Houghton Mifflin Harcourt Publishing Company. All rights reserved.

Name _____

Words to Know

Circle the correct word to complete each sentence.

1. Fran ate her beets (these, first).

2. Beets are planted in the (ground, sometimes).

3. (Food, Sometimes) Fran eats salad, too.

4. Fran has to eat all the (food, your) on her plate.

5. "Eat (ground, your) peas," said Mom.

6. The peas are (your, right) from the shop.

7. Fran looked (under, first) her peas.

8. Fran said, "(These, Under) peas look good!"

© Houghton Mifflin Harcourt Publishing Company. All rights reserved.

Name _____

Words with *ai*, *ay*

Where Does Food Come From?
Phonics: Words with *ai, ay*

Read the words. Circle the word that names the picture.

1.

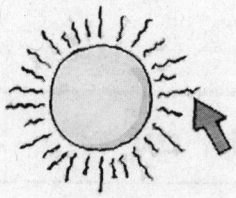

tray ray

2.

sail tail

3.

may play

4.

rain main

5.

paint pant

© Houghton Mifflin Harcourt Publishing Company. All rights reserved.

Where Does Food Come From?
Spelling: Words with *ai, ay*

Name _____

Spelling Words with the Vowel Pairs *ai*, *ay*

Sort the words. Write the correct Spelling Words in each column.

Words with ai	Words with ay
_____	_____
_____	_____
_____	_____
_____	_____
_____	_____
_____	_____
_____	_____
_____	_____
_____	_____
_____	_____
_____	_____
_____	_____
_____	_____
_____	_____
_____	_____

Spelling Words

play
grain
sail
mail
may
rain
way
day
stay
pain

© Houghton Mifflin Harcourt Publishing Company. All rights reserved.

Name _____

Where Does Food Come From?
Names of Months, Days, and Holidays

Months, Days, and Holidays

Listen to the names in the Word Bank. Read along. Circle the month, day, or holiday in each sentence. Write it correctly on the line.

Word Bank

Labor Day Tuesday May June Saturday August

1. On labor day we had a picnic. _____

2. On tuesday Hank makes a cake. _____

3. We plant seeds each may. _____

Draw a line under the correct sentence in each pair.

4. Ike likes June for planting beans.
   Ike likes june for planting beans.

5. I picked beans on Saturday.
   I picked beans on saturday.

6. Peaches grow best in august.
   Peaches grow best in August.

© Houghton Mifflin Harcourt Publishing Company. All rights reserved.

Where Does Food Come From?
Writing: Narrative Writing

Name _____

Using Different Kinds of Sentences

Write a friendly letter about a special meal you had. Write statements and a question.

20

Dear _____ ,

I ate _____ with _____ .

(statement)

_____ .

(statement)

_____ ?

(question)

_____ ,

© Houghton Mifflin Harcourt Publishing Company. All rights reserved.

Name _____

Contractions *'ll, 'd*

Write a word from the box to finish each sentence.

I'd

he'd	she'll	I'd	they'll	we'd

1. Ben said that _____ be late today.

2. Beth said _____ go to the beach.

3. Mom and Dad said _____ go out at five.

4. Gus said, "_____ like to play in the sand."

5. We think _____ like a day at the beach.

© Houghton Mifflin Harcourt Publishing Company. All rights reserved.

Name _____ Date _____

Reader's Guide

Where Food Comes From

Make a Meal!

I am going to have a glass of milk and a grilled cheese sandwich with tomatoes for lunch. I need four different kinds of food. Write where each food comes from. Look at pages 98–99, 104–105, and 107 for text evidence to help you.

1. Milk comes from _____

2. Bread comes from _____

3. Cheese comes from _____

4. Tomatoes come from _____

© Houghton Mifflin Harcourt Publishing Company. All rights reserved.

Name _____ Date _____

Where Does Food Come From?
Independent Reading

Now it's time for breakfast! Draw foods on the plate. Label them. Write a sentence telling where each food comes from. Look in the selection for text evidence to help you.

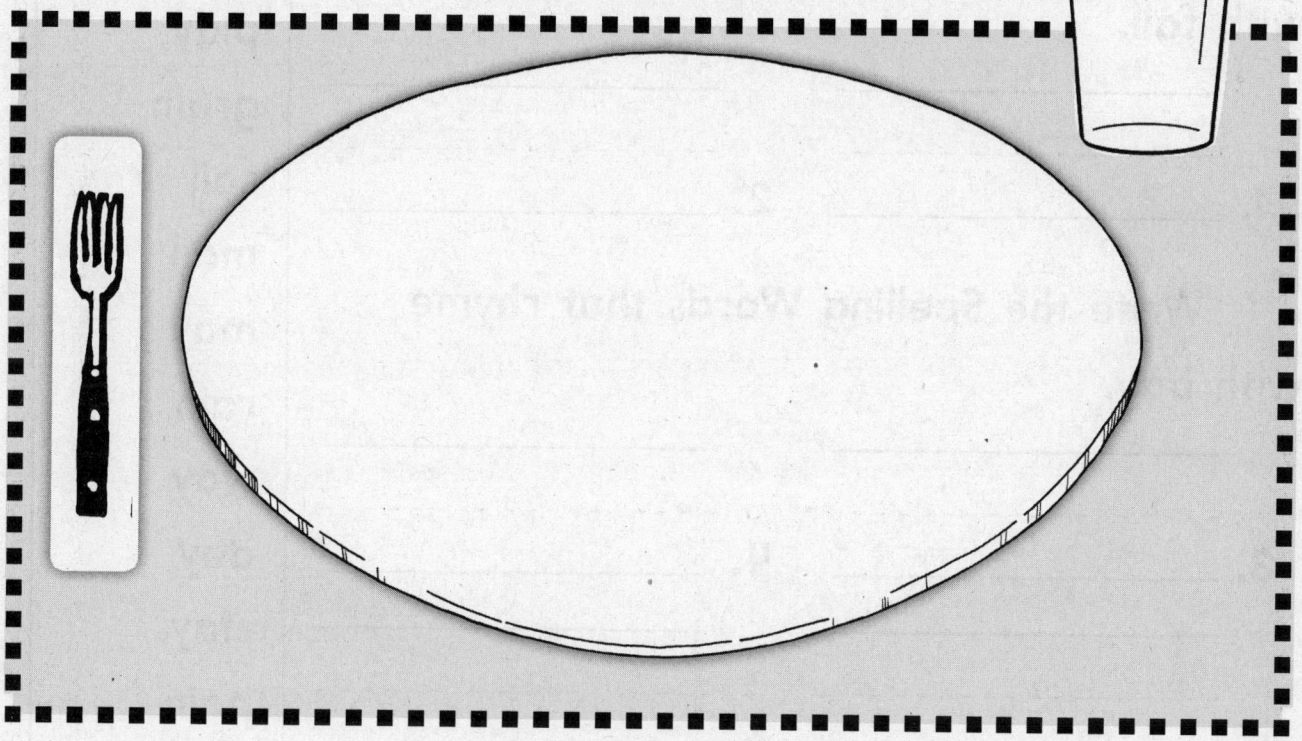

© Houghton Mifflin Harcourt Publishing Company. All rights reserved.

Name _____

Where Does Food Come From?
Spelling: Words with *ai, ay*

Spelling Words with the Vowel Pairs *ai*, *ay*

Spelling Words

play
grain
sail
mail
may
rain
way
day
stay
pain

Write the Spelling Words that rhyme with **fail.**

1. _____ 2. _____

Write the Spelling Words that rhyme with **bay.**

3. _____ 4. _____

5. _____ 6. _____

7. _____

Write the Spelling Words that rhyme with **main.**

8. _____ 9. _____ 10. _____

© Houghton Mifflin Harcourt Publishing Company. All rights reserved.

Name _____

Commas in Dates

Where Does Food Come From?

Grammar: Names of Months, Days, and Holidays

Circle the comma in each date.

1. Ms. Ray moved to the farm on October 25, 2001.
2. She planted wheat on March 13, 2010.
3. She got some chicks on May 28, 2011.
4. She had eggs for sale on June 4, 2012.

The date in each sentence is underlined. Write the date correctly.

5. This patch was planted on <u>march 16 2012</u>.

_____

_____

6. The peas were planted on <u>april 23 2012</u>.

_____

_____

© Houghton Mifflin Harcourt Publishing Company. All rights reserved.

Name _____

Where Does Food Come From?
Writing: Narrative Writing

Planning My Letter

Write and draw details that tell what happened first, next, and last.

I will write my letter to _____.

I will tell about _____.

First

Next

Last

© Houghton Mifflin Harcourt Publishing Company. All rights reserved.

Name _____

Where Does Food Come From?
Spelling: Words with Long *a*

Spelling Words with the Long *a* Sound

Write the correct word to complete each sentence.

1. Can you come out and _____?

play **clay**

_____

2. In April there is a lot of _____.

rake **rain**

_____

3. Let us _____ on the lake.

sail **tail**

_____

4. I feel a _____ in my leg.

train **pain**

_____

5. Wheat is a _____.

grain **green**

© Houghton Mifflin Harcourt Publishing Company. All rights reserved.

Name _____

Spiral Review

Circle the correct verb. Then write the sentence with the correct verb.

1. The kids (walk, walks) around the pond.

_____

_____

2. Nine sheep (eat, eats) the grass.

_____

_____

3. Ducks (flap, flaps) their wings.

_____

_____

4. One mule (sleep, sleeps) in the hay.

_____

_____

5. Pigs (play, plays) in the mud.

_____

_____

© Houghton Mifflin Harcourt Publishing Company. All rights reserved.

Name _____

Grammar in Writing

Where Does Food Come From?
Grammar: Names of Months, Days and Holidays

The name of each **month, day,** and **holiday** begins with a capital letter. When you write a date, use a **comma** between the day of the month and the year.

Example:

labor day is monday september 7 2012.

Listen to the names of months and holidays in the Word Bank. Read along. Fix the mistakes in these sentences. Use proofreading marks.

Word Bank

July **August** **September** **October**
December **New Year's Eve**

1. In october it was cold.
2. Mr. Potts left on august 22 2004.
3. Every september they sell jam.
4. Ms. Down opened the shop on july 18 2012.
5. new year's eve is on december 31.

Proofreading Marks			
^	Add	≡	Capital letter

© Houghton Mifflin Harcourt Publishing Company. All rights reserved.

Name _____

Tomás Rivera
Phonics: Words with *oa, ow*

Words with *oa, ow*

Read the word. Circle the picture that matches the word.

1.

boat

2.

crow

3.

goat

4.

bowl

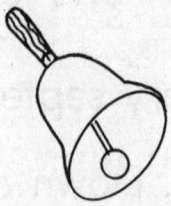

5.

loaf

© Houghton Mifflin Harcourt Publishing Company. All rights reserved.

Name _____

Words to Know

Tomás Rivera
High-Frequency Words

Listen to the clues. Read along. Circle the best answer to each clue.

1. This means **finished**.	**paper**	**done**
2. This is in a short while.	**soon**	**great**
3. This means **speak**.	**were**	**talk**
4. **Awful** is its opposite.	**great**	**soon**
5. A joke makes you do this.	**laugh**	**done**
6. You write on this.	**work**	**paper**
7. This is a **job**.	**great**	**work**
8. Past tense for **are**.	**laugh**	**were**

© Houghton Mifflin Harcourt Publishing Company. All rights reserved.

Name _____

Words with *oa*, *ow*

Circle the two words in each row that rhyme. Then write the letters that stand for the long o sound.

1.

grow blow block gray

_____ _____

2.

slow sling throw thick

_____ _____

3.

much road load lunch

_____ _____

4.

coat got goat long

_____ _____

5.

flame show ground snow

_____ _____

© Houghton Mifflin Harcourt Publishing Company. All rights reserved.

Name _____

Tomás Rivera
Spelling: Words with *oa, ow*

Spelling Words with Vowel Pairs *oa, ow*

Sort the words. Write the correct Spelling Words in each column.

Words with ow	Words with oa

Spelling Words

show
row
boat
blow
toad
road
low
coat
grow
snow

© Houghton Mifflin Harcourt Publishing Company. All rights reserved.

Name _____

Tomás Rivera
Grammar: Verbs and Time

Future Using *will*

Circle the sentences that tell about the future. Rewrite the other sentences to tell about the future using *will*.

1. I read each day.

2. Brent will meet you at the shop.

3. My dad helps me read.

4. They washed the van.

5. Fran will beat the eggs.

_____

6. _____

_____

7. _____

_____

8. _____

_____

_____

© Houghton Mifflin Harcourt Publishing Company. All rights reserved.

Name _____

Tomás Rivera
Writing: Narrative Writing

Order of Events

Draw pictures to show what you did to get ready for school today.

Write sentences about what you did to get ready for school today.

First, _____

Next, _____

Last, _____

© Houghton Mifflin Harcourt Publishing Company. All rights reserved.

Name _____

Tomás Rivera
Phonics: Contractions *'ve, 're*

Contractions *'ve, 're*

Draw a line from each pair of words to its contraction.

You are	You're
They have	I've
I have	We're
We are	They've

Write a sentence using one of the contractions from above.

_____

_____

_____

_____

© Houghton Mifflin Harcourt Publishing Company. All rights reserved.

Name _____

Contractions *'ve, 're*

Write the contraction that finishes each sentence.

1. _____ all set for our big game.
   We are

2. _____ my best friend.
   You are

3. _____ had a lot of fun today!
   I have

4. _____ had a lot of rain.
   They have

© Houghton Mifflin Harcourt Publishing Company. All rights reserved.

Name _____ Date _____

Tomás Rivera

Introducing Tomás Rivera

Let's make a sign for the Tomás Rivera Library!

Read pages 134–138. Tell people what was important to Tomás Rivera. Tell why the library has his name.

The Tomás Rivera Library

© Houghton Mifflin Harcourt Publishing Company. All rights reserved.

Name _____ Date _____

Tomás Rivera
Independent Reading

Read pages 139–141. Draw something that was important to Tomás Rivera. Write a caption for your drawing to tell why it was important.

© Houghton Mifflin Harcourt Publishing Company. All rights reserved.

Tomás Rivera
Spelling: Words with *oa, ow*

Name _____

Spelling Words with Vowel Pairs *oa, ow*

Write the Spelling Word that fits each clue.

1. Opposite of **high** _____

2. Another word for **street** _____

3. You watch this on TV. _____

4. You see this in winter. _____

5. Wear this in the cold. _____

6. An animal _____

Spelling Words

show
row
grow
low
blow
snow
boat
coat
road
toad

© Houghton Mifflin Harcourt Publishing Company. All rights reserved.

Name _____

Tomás Rivera
Grammar: Verbs and Time

Future Using *going to*

Circle the sentences that tell about the future. Rewrite the other sentences to tell about the future. Use going to in each one.

1. I work with Ed.
2. Ed is going to have many crops.
3. My dad planted beets.
4. They pulled the weeds.
5. Jen is going to pick beans with Sam.
6. Tess has a pet cat.

_____

7. _____

_____

8. _____

_____

9. _____

_____

10. _____

© Houghton Mifflin Harcourt Publishing Company. All rights reserved.

Name _____

Tomás Rivera
Spelling: Words with Long *o*

Spelling Words with the Long *o* Sound

Write the correct word to complete each sentence.

_____

1. The class will put on a _____.

show **snow**

_____

2. The _____ hopped on the grass.

toad **load**

_____

3. How do plants _____?

throw **grow**

_____

4. The _____ came in with fish.

boat **bat**

_____

5. Which _____ will you sit in?

row **read**

© Houghton Mifflin Harcourt Publishing Company. All rights reserved.

Name _____

Spiral Review

Notice the clue word yesterday that tells about the past. Circle the verb that tells about the past. Then write those verbs.

1. **Yesterday** mom (works, worked) at the new shop. _____
2. She (opens, opened) the shop at nine. _____
3. Many kids (walk, walked) into the shop. _____
4. Val (asks, asked) for a new game. _____
5. Her mom (helps, helped) her. _____

© Houghton Mifflin Harcourt Publishing Company. All rights reserved.

Name _____

Tomás Rivera
Writing: Narrative Writing

Planning My Personal Narrative

Draw and write details that tell what happened first, next, and last.

My Topic: _____

First

Next

Last

© Houghton Mifflin Harcourt Publishing Company. All rights reserved.

Name _____

Tomás Rivera
Grammar: Verbs and Time

Grammar in Writing

You can write sentences that tell what may happen in the future. Use **will** or **is going to** to write sentences about the future.

Example: Jill walks.

Jill **will** walk.

Jill **is going to** walk.

Rewrite each sentence to tell about the future.

1. Tom runs far.

_____

_____

2. He went to work.

_____

_____

3. Grandpa sails his boat.

_____

_____

_____

_____

© Houghton Mifflin Harcourt Publishing Company. All rights reserved.

Name _____

Little Rabbit's Tale
Phonics: Compound Words

Compound Words

Name each picture. Circle two words to make a compound for the picture. Write the compound word.

1.

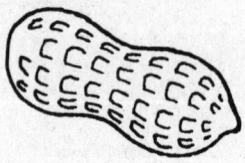

sea pea _____

nut side _____

2.

trail rain _____

bow mix _____

3.

blue sea _____

bird shell _____

4.

snow mail _____

box flake _____

5.

cup sail _____

cake boat _____

© Houghton Mifflin Harcourt Publishing Company. All rights reserved.

Name _____

Words to Know

Little Rabbit's Tale
High-Frequency Words

Circle the best answer to each question.

1. What word goes with **less**? more use
2. What word goes with **dry**? door wash
3. What word goes with **open**? want door
4. What word goes with **father**? mother more
5. What word goes with **new**? old wash
6. What word goes with **need**? wash want
7. What word goes with **test**? more try
8. What word goes with **tools**? use mother

© Houghton Mifflin Harcourt Publishing Company. All rights reserved.

Name _____

Little Rabbit's Tale
Phonics: Compound Words

Compound Words

Choose words from the box to make a compound word to name each picture. Write the word. You will use some words more than once.

mail	rain	sail	sand	bow
row	boat	coat	box	

1. 

2. 

3. 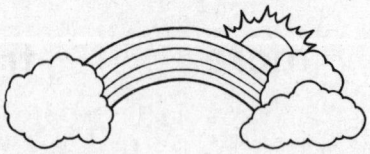

4. 

5. 

6. 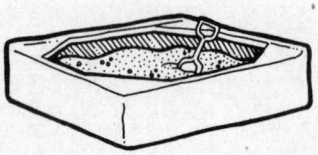

© Houghton Mifflin Harcourt Publishing Company. All rights reserved.

Name _____

Little Rabbit's Tale
Spelling: Compound Words

Spelling Compound Words

Write the two words that make up each Spelling Word shown below.

1. bedtime _____ _____
2. himself _____ _____
3. flagpole _____ _____
4. sailboat _____ _____
5. backpack _____ _____
6. sunset _____ _____
7. raincoat _____ _____

© Houghton Mifflin Harcourt Publishing Company. All rights reserved.

Name _____

Little Rabbit's Tale
Grammar: Prepositions

Prepositional Phrases for Where

Circle the prepositional phase in each sentence. Write it on the line.

1. Rabbit went to Squirrel's home.

_____

_____

2. He went up the steps.

_____

_____

3. He knocked on the door.

_____

_____

Complete each sentence. Write a prepositional phrase that tells where.

4. The rabbit lives _____.

_____

_____

5. The rabbit hopped _____.

© Houghton Mifflin Harcourt Publishing Company. All rights reserved.

Name _____

Little Rabbit's Tale
Writing: Narrative Writing

Exact Details

Read each underlined detail. Write a more exact detail to finish each sentence.

1. I watched <u>an animal</u>.

_____

I watched _____.

2. I fed it <u>some food</u>.

_____

I fed it _____.

3. It <u>moved around</u>.

_____

It _____.

4. I will teach it <u>something</u>.

_____

I will teach it _____.

© Houghton Mifflin Harcourt Publishing Company. All rights reserved.

Name _____

Little Rabbit's Tale
Phonics: Short *e* Sound Spelled *ea*

Words with Short Vowel /ĕ/*ea*

Circle two words that have the short e sound.

1.

red bread bat rode

2.

sled bone robe head

3.

bed dead cube lot

4.

peach fed Fred drink

5.

led paint loaf thread

© Houghton Mifflin Harcourt Publishing Company. All rights reserved.

Name _____ Date _____

Reader's Guide

Little Rabbit's Tale

Goose and Beaver Tell the Tale

It is time for Goose and Beaver to tell the story!

Read pages 164–169. Tell this part of the story the way Goose would tell it. Tell how Goose feels and what happens.

© Houghton Mifflin Harcourt Publishing Company. All rights reserved.

Name _____ Date _____

Little Rabbit's Tale
Independent Reading

Read pages 174–179. Tell the end of the story like Beaver would tell it. Why is Beaver unhappy at Little Rabbit's house? What happens next?

© Houghton Mifflin Harcourt Publishing Company. All rights reserved.

Name _____

Little Rabbit's Tale
Spelling: Compound Words

Spelling Compound Words

Draw a line from a word on the left to a word on the right to make each Spelling Word.

1. bath	time
2. flag	tub
3. bed	pole
4. sun	pack
5. back	set
6. play	coat
7. rain	pen
8. sail	side
9. in	self
10. him	boat

Spelling Words

bedtime
sunset
bathtub
sailboat
flagpole
backpack
playpen
raincoat
inside
himself

© Houghton Mifflin Harcourt Publishing Company. All rights reserved.

Name _____

Little Rabbit's Tale
Grammar: Prepositions

Prepositional Phrases

Circle the prepositional phrase in each sentence. Decide if the prepositional phrase tells where or when. Write where or when on the line.

1. The friends play after lunch. _____

2. They meet at Viv's home. _____

3. Viv swings under a tree. _____

4. Lin skips on the grass. _____

5. Mom comes home at five o'clock. _____

6. Lin goes home before then. _____

© Houghton Mifflin Harcourt Publishing Company. All rights reserved.

Name _____

Spelling Compound Words

Write the correct word to complete each sentence.

1. The _____ was very red.

   sunset himself

2. Let us play _____ today.

   inside flagpole

3. I carry my _____ with me.

   playpen backpack

4. Before _____ I brush my teeth.

   bedtime sailboat

5. My _____ has a matching hat.

   bathtub raincoat

© Houghton Mifflin Harcourt Publishing Company. All rights reserved.

Name _____

Spiral Review

Write each sentence with the correct verb.

1. This puppet (is, are) small.

_____

_____

2. Raindrops (is, are) wet.

_____

_____

3. The lambs (is, are) white.

_____

_____

4. The show (was, were) funny.

_____

_____

5. Those muffins (was, were) huge.

_____

_____

© Houghton Mifflin Harcourt Publishing Company. All rights reserved.

Name _____

Grammar in Writing

Little Rabbit's Tale
Grammar: Prepositions

A prepositional phrase can tell when or where.

Example: We walk **after lunch**. when
We walk **in the park**. where

Add a prepositional phrase to each sentence to tell when or where. Write the new sentence on the line.

1. My friends and I ran.

_____

2. Something fell.

_____

3. I tripped.

_____

4. I went home.

_____

© Houghton Mifflin Harcourt Publishing Company. All rights reserved.

Name _____ Date _____

Amazing Whales!

What I Know About Whales

Draw your favorite whale. Label your picture.
Tell one fact that makes this whale amazing.

Kind of whale

_____

_____

Amazing Fact

_____

_____

© Houghton Mifflin Harcourt Publishing Company. All rights reserved.

Name _____ Date _____

Amazing Whales!
Read Aloud

Whales are in trouble! Write three things people can do to help them.

1.

2.

3.

© Houghton Mifflin Harcourt Publishing Company. All rights reserved.

Name _____

The Garden
Phonics: *r*-Controlled Vowel *ar*

Words with *ar*

Circle the word that matches the picture.

1.

cat card

2.

star stamp

3.

march much

4.

barn bark

5.

arm art

6.

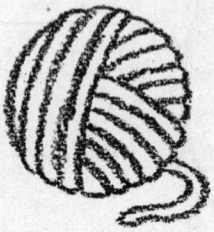

yard yarn

© Houghton Mifflin Harcourt Publishing Company. All rights reserved.

Name _____

Words to Know

Circle the correct word to complete each sentence.

1. Dad reads us a funny (story, noise).

2. The children are making a lot of (loudly, noise).

3. Tim's parents are planning a trip around the (world, window).

4. Those children are talking (loudly, story) in class.

5. I (few, shall) be late for school tomorrow.

6. Some animals hunt at (night, world).

7. Close your (night, window) when it rains.

8. (Few, Shall) birds can swim.

© Houghton Mifflin Harcourt Publishing Company. All rights reserved.

Name _____

The Garden
Phonics: *r*-Controlled Vowel *ar*

Words with *ar*

Look at the picture and read the words.
Write the word that matches the picture.

1.

stem start

_____

2.

cat cart

_____

3.

car card

_____

4.

shake shark

_____

5.

pack park

_____

© Houghton Mifflin Harcourt Publishing Company. All rights reserved.

Name _____

The Garden
Spelling: Words with *ar*

Spelling Words with *r*-Controlled Vowel *ar*

Spelling Words

far
arm
yard
art
jar
bar
barn
bark
card
yarn

Write the Spelling Words that rhyme with far, yard, and barn.

1. **Far** rhymes with _____ and _____.

2. **Yard** rhymes with _____.

3. **Barn** rhymes with _____.

Write the Spelling Word that names the picture.

4. 

_____

5. 

_____

6. 

_____

© Houghton Mifflin Harcourt Publishing Company. All rights reserved.

Name _____

The Garden
Grammar: Subject Pronouns

Pronouns That Name One

Circle the pronoun that can take the place of the underlined word or words.

1. Grandpa makes a shed.

He **She** **It**

2. The shed is short and wide.

He **She** **It**

3. Ann helps Grandpa work in the shed.

He **She** **It**

Write He, She, or It to take the place of the underlined word or words.

4. Joe sees a nest.

_____ sees a nest.

5. The nest has eggs.

_____ has eggs.

© Houghton Mifflin Harcourt Publishing Company. All rights reserved.

Name _____

The Garden
Writing: Narrative Writing

Dialogue

Think of another problem that Toad could have with his garden. Then write what he and Frog might have said.

Toad still needed help with his garden. He asked Frog what "_____ to do. _____ ?" Toad asked. "_____ ," said Frog.

© Houghton Mifflin Harcourt Publishing Company. All rights reserved.

Name _____

The Garden

Phonics: *r*-Controlled Vowels *or, ore*

Words with *or, ore*

Read the sentences. Circle the sentence that tells about the picture.

1. We look at the score.

We look at the star.

2. I like to do chores.

I snore when I sleep.

3. She finds shells at the shore.

She finds fish at the shop.

4. He can play the thorn.

He can play the horn.

5. Here is a jar.

Here is a fork.

© Houghton Mifflin Harcourt Publishing Company. All rights reserved.

Name _____ Date _____

Reader's Guide

The Garden

Could That Really Happen?

Think about the story and what could happen in real life.

Read pages 15–18. Read what happens. Decide if it could happen in real life. Tell why or why not.

What Happens	Could this happen in real life? Why or why not?
A frog and toad talk to each other.	
The seeds did not grow right after they were put in the ground.	

© Houghton Mifflin Harcourt Publishing Company. All rights reserved.

Name _____ Date _____

The Garden
Independent Reading

Read pages 19–29. Fill in the chart.

What Happens	Could this happen in real life? Why or why not?
Frog said that shouting at the seeds kept them from growing.	
The seeds were afraid of the dark.	
Letting the sun shine on the seeds and the rain fall on them helped them grow.	

© Houghton Mifflin Harcourt Publishing Company. All rights reserved.

Name _____

Spelling Words with *r*-Controlled Vowel *ar*

Write the Spelling Word that names the picture.

Spelling Words

far
arm
yard
art
jar
bar
barn
bark
card
yarn

1.

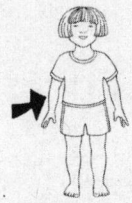

_____

2.

_____

3.

_____

4.

_____

5.

_____

6.

_____

© Houghton Mifflin Harcourt Publishing Company. All rights reserved.

Name _____

The Garden
Grammar: Subject Pronouns

Pronouns That Name More Than One

Circle the pronoun that can take the place of each underlined subject.

1. Workers plant trees in the park.

   We **They**

2. The trees grow big.

   We **They**

3. Sis and I sit under the trees.

   We **They**

Write We or They to take the place of each underlined subject.

4. Dad and I walk to the park.

   _____ walk to the park.

5. Pete and Kate run and play.

   _____ run and play.

© Houghton Mifflin Harcourt Publishing Company. All rights reserved.

Name _____

The Garden
Writing: Narrative Writing

Planning My Sentences

Write and draw details that tell what happened first and next.

Topic: After Toad's garden started to grow,

_____

Frog and Toad _____.

First

Next

© Houghton Mifflin Harcourt Publishing Company. All rights reserved.

Name _____

The Garden
Spelling: Words with *ar*

Spelling Words with *r*-Controlled Vowel *ar*

Write the correct word to complete each sentence.

fun	far

1. She lives _____ away from me.

ants	arm

2. He waves his _____ in the air.

yard	yarn

3. We play in the _____.

art	part

4. We paint in _____ class.

bar	jar

5. She gave me a _____ of jam.

card	bar

6. Hang your coats on the _____.

barn	big

7. The sheep are in the _____.

© Houghton Mifflin Harcourt Publishing Company. All rights reserved.

Name _____

Spiral Review

Draw a line under each question.

1. What sort of tree is this?
2. Do all trees have leaves?
3. Pine trees have cones.
4. What animals live in trees?
5. Birds live in trees.
6. Do we need trees?
7. Trees give us air.
8. Do we get food from trees?

© Houghton Mifflin Harcourt Publishing Company. All rights reserved.

Name _____

Grammar in Writing

The Garden
Grammar: Subject Pronouns

The pronouns **he, she,** and **it** name one. The pronouns **we** and **they** name more than one.

Fix the mistakes in the sentences. Use proofreading marks.

Example: The shed is done. ~~She~~ It looks nice.

1. Mom saws. He makes a shelf for the shed.

2. Bob and I get paint. They paint the shelf.

3. Mom has some grapes. It puts them in a bowl.

4. My friends come over. We want to see the shed.

Proofreading Marks	
^	add
⁓	take out

© Houghton Mifflin Harcourt Publishing Company. All rights reserved.

Name _____

Amazing Animals
Phonics: *r*-Controlled Vowels *er, ir, ur*

Words with *er, ir, ur*

Read the word. Circle the picture that matches the word.

1. bird		
2. turn		
3. her		
4. burn		
5. third		
6. herd		

© Houghton Mifflin Harcourt Publishing Company. All rights reserved.

Name _____

Words to Know

Circle the word that best completes each sentence.

1. I like (until, learning) about animals.

2. Our dog Pip is five (follow, years) old.

3. Pip has (baby, eight) new pups.

4. She will feed her pups (until, learning) they are older.

5. A (eight, young) kitten came to our home.

6. The new kitten likes to (until, follow) Pip.

7. The kitten (begins, learning) to think he is Pip's pup!

8. The new kitten is not Pip's (years, baby).

© Houghton Mifflin Harcourt Publishing Company. All rights reserved.

Name _____

Amazing Animals
Phonics: *r*-Controlled Vowels *er, ir, ur*

Words with *er, ir, ur*

Read the words in the box. Write the word that matches the picture.

clerk	shirt	stir	hurt	curl

1. 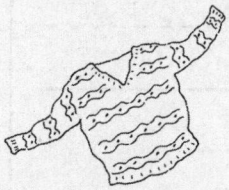

2. 

3. 

4. 

5. 

© Houghton Mifflin Harcourt Publishing Company. All rights reserved.

Name _____

Amazing Animals
Spelling: Words with *er, ir, ur*

Spelling Words with *r*-Controlled Vowels *er*, *ir*, *ur*

Spelling Words

sir
fern
girl
her
third
hurt
fur
bird
turn
stir

Write the Spelling Words with **er**.

1. _____
2. _____

Write the Spelling Words with **ir**.

3. _____
4. _____
5. _____
6. _____
7. _____

Write the Spelling Words with **ur**.

8. _____
9. _____
10. _____

© Houghton Mifflin Harcourt Publishing Company. All rights reserved.

Name _____

Naming Yourself Last

Amazing Animals
Grammar: The Pronouns *I* and *Me*

Circle the correct words to finish each sentence.

1. _____ see the goat.

Jean and me **Jean and I**

2. Dad took _____ to the zoo.

I and Steve **Steve and me**

3. _____ look at the ducks.

Rex and I **Rex and me**

Write the words from the word box to finish the sentence.

Ann	I

4. _____ and _____ hold the baby snakes.

© Houghton Mifflin Harcourt Publishing Company. All rights reserved.

Name _____

Amazing Animals
Writing: Narrative Writing

Exact Verbs

Draw a picture of an animal for a story. Give your animal a name.

_____

Name: _____

Finish these story sentences about your animal. Use exact verbs.

_____ _____ is a _____ _____ .
name kind of animal

_____ _____ likes to _____ _____ .
name exact verb

_____ _____ always _____ _____ a lot!
name exact verb

© Houghton Mifflin Harcourt Publishing Company. All rights reserved.

Name _____

Amazing Animals
Phonics: *r*-Controlled Vowels *er, ir, ur*

Words with *er, ir, ur*

Choose a word from the box to name each picture. Write the word.

girl	turn	chirp	third	hers	dirt

1.

_____

_____

2.

_____

_____

3.

_____

_____

4.

_____

_____

5.

_____

_____

6.

_____

_____

© Houghton Mifflin Harcourt Publishing Company. All rights reserved.

Name _____ Date _____

Reader's Guide

Amazing Animals

Where Is My Home?

The animals got mixed up! Write where each animal lives. Then, write the clues you used to figure out the answer.

pond	ocean	arctic	desert	grassland

Read pages 48–50.
Where is the bear's home? _____
What clues did you use?

_____

_____

_____

Read pages 51–54. Where is the camel's home? _____
What clues did you use?

_____

_____

_____

© Houghton Mifflin Harcourt Publishing Company. All rights reserved.

Name _____ Date _____

Amazing Animals
Independent Reading

Read pages 55–56.
Where is the duck's home?
What clues did you use?

Read pages 57–58.
Where is the giraffe's home?
What clues did you use?

Read pages 59–65.
Where is the dolphin's home? What clues did you use?

© Houghton Mifflin Harcourt Publishing Company. All rights reserved.

Name _____

Amazing Animals
Spelling: Words with *er, ir, ur*

Spelling Words with *r*-Controlled Vowels *er*, *ir*, *ur*

Spelling Words

her
fern
girl
sir
stir
bird
fur
hurt
turn
third

Write the Spelling Word that fits each clue.

1. Opposite of **boy** _____
2. Goes with **pain** _____
3. What a bear has _____
4. Goes with **three** _____
5. Opposite of **him** _____
6. An animal _____

© Houghton Mifflin Harcourt Publishing Company. All rights reserved.

Name _____

Naming Yourself with *I*

Amazing Animals
Grammar: The Pronouns *I* and *Me*

Write the sentences correctly.

1. Jay and me visit a farm.

2. Me and Bree feed the ducks.

3. Dave and me pet the sheep.

4. Me and Ed see the lambs.

5. Meg and me hold the cat.

© Houghton Mifflin Harcourt Publishing Company. All rights reserved.

Name _____

Amazing Animals
Writing: Narrative Writing

Planning My Sentences

Write and draw details that tell what happened first and next.

My Topic: I will write about a

_____

_____

_____

First

Next

This is how my story will end:

© Houghton Mifflin Harcourt Publishing Company. All rights reserved.

Name _____

Amazing Animals
Spelling: Words with *r*-Controlled Vowels *er, ir, ur*

Spelling Words with *r*-Controlled Vowels *er, ir, ur*

Spelling Words

her
fern
stir
fur
hurt
turn
third
girl
sir
bird

Write the Spelling Word that completes each sentence.

1. I like _____ dress.
2. I watered the _____.
3. The _____ has a pink doll.
4. I fell and _____ my arm.
5. The _____ laid three eggs.
6. The cat has thick _____.

© Houghton Mifflin Harcourt Publishing Company. All rights reserved.

Name _____

Spiral Review

Draw a line under the two shorter sentences in each compound sentence.

1. Can we go to the zoo, or is it too cold?
2. I want to see the ducks, but they want to see the foxes.
3. Sit quietly, and eat your snack.

Write a compound sentence by combining the two shorter sentences.

4. Dad baked a cake. We helped him.

_____

and

_____

_____

_____

© Houghton Mifflin Harcourt Publishing Company. All rights reserved.

Name _____

Amazing Animals
Grammar: The Pronouns *I* and *Me*

Grammar in Writing

Use the pronoun **I** in the subject of a sentence. Use the pronoun **me** in the predicate of a sentence. Name yourself last.

Fix the mistakes in these sentences. Use proofreading marks.

Example: Ted ~~Me~~ and I ~~Ted~~ see the ducklings.

1. I and Mark feed the pups.

2. Mom helps me and Jon at the zoo.

3. Me and Hing look at the piglets.

4. Kris and i see the baby birds.

Proofreading Marks	
^	add
~~	take out
≡	capital letter

© Houghton Mifflin Harcourt Publishing Company. All rights reserved.

Name _____

Whistle for Willie
Phonics: Vowel Digraph /o͝o/*oo*

The Vowel Sound *oo* *(book)*

Circle the word that matches the picture.

1.

book hook

2.

book cook

3.

wool wood

4.

hook hood

5.

brook took

6.

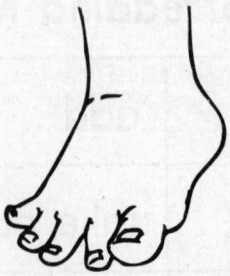

soot foot

© Houghton Mifflin Harcourt Publishing Company. All rights reserved.

Name _____

Words to Know

Whistle for Willie
High-Frequency Words

Circle the word that best completes each sentence.

1. We can go to the play (together, boy).

2. The box has (began, nothing) in it.

3. The new (boy, along) is named Dan.

4. Dan and his (together, father) like to fish.

5. My (house, nothing) has a blue door.

6. Jan skipped (house, along) the path.

7. I will sing the song (again, boy).

8. A bell (house, began) to ring.

© Houghton Mifflin Harcourt Publishing Company. All rights reserved.

Name _____

Whistle for Willie
Phonics: Vowel Digraph /o͝o/*oo*

Words with *oo (book)*

Circle the sentence that matches the picture.

1. We cook at mealtime.

We look at the time.

2. I see a little brook.

I see a little book.

3. He has a hat made of wool.

He has a box made of wood.

4. Put your coat on a hook.

Put your coat in a hood.

5. Wash off that soot.

Wash off your foot.

© Houghton Mifflin Harcourt Publishing Company. All rights reserved.

Name _____

Whistle for Willie
Spelling: Words with *oo*

Spelling Words with Vowel Digraph *oo*

Sort the words. Write the correct Spelling Words in each column.

Words with **ook**	Words with **ood**

Spelling Words

look
book
good
hook
brook
took
foot
shook
wood
hood

© Houghton Mifflin Harcourt Publishing Company. All rights reserved.

Name _____

Whistle for Willie
Grammar: Possessive Pronouns

Using *my*, *your*, *his*, and *her*

Write the correct pronoun to finish each sentence.

1. I hug _____ dog Mags.

me **my**

2. Mags runs after _____ stick.

her **she**

3. Rick brings _____ dog.

he **his**

4. You can bring _____ dog, too.

your **you**

5. We can play in _____ backyard!

they **my**

© Houghton Mifflin Harcourt Publishing Company. All rights reserved.

Name _____

Order of Events

Whistle for Willie
Writing: Narrative Writing

Finish the sentences. Give a summary of the first part of Whistle for Willie.

Peter wished _____.

He tried _____.

When Peter saw Willie, he _____.

Then, Willie _____.

© Houghton Mifflin Harcourt Publishing Company. All rights reserved.

Name _____

Whistle for Willie
Phonics: Syllable Pattern CVC

How Many Syllables?

Read each word. Circle how many syllables it has. Hint: Each time you hear a vowel sound, there is a syllable.

1.

hammer
1 2

2.

doctor
1 2

3.

stood
1 2

4.

rabbit
1 2

5.

mister
1 2

6.

third
1 2

© Houghton Mifflin Harcourt Publishing Company. All rights reserved.

Name _____ Date _____

Whistle for Willie

Picture Words

Good readers make pictures in their mind as they read.

Read pages 83–87. Draw what Peter is doing on page 86. Write the words that help you picture it.

© Houghton Mifflin Harcourt Publishing Company. All rights reserved.

Name _____ Date _____

Whistle for Willie
Independent Reading

Read pages 88–91. Do you see the cat? Write how the cat might describe what it sees and hears Peter doing.

Read pages 92–103. Then look back at pages 96–97. Write how Willie might describe what he sees and hears.

© Houghton Mifflin Harcourt Publishing Company. All rights reserved.

Name _____

Whistle for Willie
Spelling: Words with *oo*

Spelling Words with Vowel Digraph *oo*

Write each group of Spelling Words in ABC order.

look	hood	shook	hook
good	wood	foot	brook
book		took	
_____		_____	
_____		_____	
_____		_____	
_____		_____	
_____		_____	
_____		_____	
_____		_____	
_____		_____	
_____		_____	
_____		_____	
_____		_____	
_____		_____	
_____		_____	
_____		_____	

Spelling Words

look
book
good
hook
brook
took
foot
shook
wood
hood

© Houghton Mifflin Harcourt Publishing Company. All rights reserved.

Name _____

Whistle for Willie
Grammar: Possessive Pronouns

Using *mine*, *yours*, *his*, and *hers*

Write the correct pronoun to finish each sentence.

1. This mitt is _____.
   your yours

2. The bat is _____.
   he his

3. That treat is _____.
   you yours

4. This house is _____.
   my mine

5. That dog is _____.
   hers her

© Houghton Mifflin Harcourt Publishing Company. All rights reserved.

Name _____

Whistle for Willie
Writing: Narrative Writing

Planning My Summary

Write sentences and draw details for your summary of Whistle for Willie.

My Topic: _____

© Houghton Mifflin Harcourt Publishing Company. All rights reserved.

Name _____

Whistle for Willie
Spelling: Words with *oo*

Spelling Words with the *oo* Sound in *book*

Spelling Words

book
look
good
hook
brook
foot
took
shook
wood
hood

Write the Spelling Words that make sense in each sentence.

1. Can I _____ at your _____ _____?

2. I _____ the _____ _____ off his coat.

3. I put my _____ in the _____ _____.

© Houghton Mifflin Harcourt Publishing Company. All rights reserved.

Name _____

Spiral Review

Listen to the names of months in the Word Bank. Read along. Write each date correctly.

Word Bank

February March August October December

1. The pet shop opened on march 13 1999.

2. Lisa got a cat on february 22 2007.

3. My dog had pups on august 1 2008.

4. His dog won a prize on october 25 2009.

5. My dog got a new bowl on december 22 2010.

© Houghton Mifflin Harcourt Publishing Company. All rights reserved.

Name _____

Whistle for Willie
Grammar: Possessive Pronouns

Grammar in Writing

- Some pronouns show that something belongs to someone.
- The pronouns **my**, **your**, **his**, and **her** come before a noun.
- The pronouns **mine**, **yours**, **his**, and **hers** come at the end of a sentence.

Fix the mistakes in these sentences. Use proofreading marks.

Example: The dog is ~~he~~ his.

1. I play with mine dog.

2. That is hers bowl.

3. This leash is your.

4. Jack has a new dog. The dog is hers.

Proofreading Marks	
^	add
——ꝏ	take out

© Houghton Mifflin Harcourt Publishing Company. All rights reserved.

Name _____

A Tree Is a Plant
Phonics: Words with *oo (moon), ou, ew*

Words with *oo (moon), ou, ew*

Circle the word that names the picture.

1.

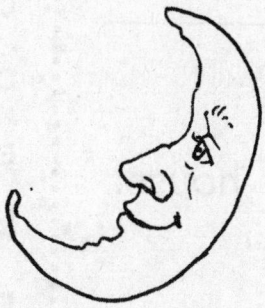

moth moon

2.

spoon spot

3.

scream screw

4.

soap soup

5.

boat boot

6.

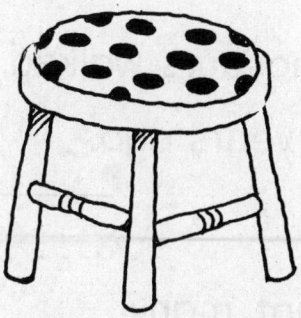

stool stole

© Houghton Mifflin Harcourt Publishing Company. All rights reserved.

Name _____

Words to Know

A Tree Is a Plant
High-Frequency Words

Write a word from the box to complete each sentence.

Words to Know

- almost
- country
- covered
- earth
- kinds
- ready
- soil
- warms

1. I planted flowers in the _____.

2. Our heater _____ our house.

3. Pete _____ hit a home run.

4. Mr. Lee lives in the _____.

5. Mom _____ us with a blanket.

6. Are you _____ to go?

7. Dinosaurs walked the _____ millions of years ago.

8. I got many _____ of games for my birthday.

© Houghton Mifflin Harcourt Publishing Company. All rights reserved.

A Tree Is a Plant
Phonics: Words with *oo (moon), ou, ew*

Name _____

Words with *oo (moon), ou, ew*

Write the word that best completes each sentence. Use the words in the Word Bank.

Word Bank

cool group room drew stool

1. I got together with a _____ of friends.
2. We had fun playing in my _____.
3. We _____ some pictures and hung them up.
4. Then we painted my old _____.
5. Now the room looks _____!

© Houghton Mifflin Harcourt Publishing Company. All rights reserved.

Name _____

A Tree Is a Plant
Spelling: Words with *oo, ou, ew*

Spelling Words with Vowel Digraphs *oo, ou, ew*

Spelling Words

soon
new
noon
zoo
boot
too
moon
blew
soup
you

Write the Spelling Words with **ou**.

1. _____
2. _____

Write the Spelling Words with **ew**.

3. _____
4. _____

Write the Spelling Words with **oo**.

5. _____
6. _____
7. _____
8. _____
9. _____
10. _____

© Houghton Mifflin Harcourt Publishing Company. All rights reserved.

Name _____

Indefinite Pronouns

Indefinite pronouns are special pronouns that stand for people or things that are not named.

Word Bank

anyone	someone	everything
something	everybody	somebody

Draw a line under the indefinite pronoun in each sentence.

1. He knows everything about trees.
2. Would anyone like an apple?
3. Someone baked apple pie.

Write an indefinite pronoun from the Word Bank to complete each sentence.

4. I learned _____ about trees.
5. Has _____ picked apples before?

© Houghton Mifflin Harcourt Publishing Company. All rights reserved.

Name _____

Describing Characters

A Tree Is a Plant
Writing: Narrative Writing

Write clear details to finish the story. Some details should describe Rex and Grace.

Rex was a _____ dog. He lived with a _____ girl named Grace. Grace liked to sit under the _____ apple tree in her yard. Grace wanted to teach Rex to _____ with her. She told Rex to _____. When Rex did the trick, Grace told Rex, "_____!" Rex wagged his _____ tail.

© Houghton Mifflin Harcourt Publishing Company. All rights reserved.

Name _____

A Tree Is a Plant
Phonics: Words with *ue, u, u_e*

Words with *ue, u, u_e*

Circle the two words in each row that have the same vowel sound.
Write the letters that stand for the sound.

				ue	u	u-e
1.	clue	trust	true	____		____
2.	prune	flute	float	____		____
3.	goal	flu	truth	____		____
4.	tone	tune	rule	____		____
5.	blue	blunt	glue	____		____

© Houghton Mifflin Harcourt Publishing Company. All rights reserved.

Name _____ Date _____

A Tree Is a Plant

Tree Diagrams

Read pages 136–137. Draw a tree with leaves and roots. Use green arrows to show how food moves. Use blue arrows to show how water moves.

© Houghton Mifflin Harcourt Publishing Company. All rights reserved.

Name _____ Date _____

A Tree Is a Plant
Independent Reading

Read pages 128–147. Draw the apple tree in each season. Start with spring. Write the name of each season.

© Houghton Mifflin Harcourt Publishing Company. All rights reserved.

Name _____

A Tree Is a Plant
Spelling: Words with *oo, ou, ew*

Spelling Words with Vowel Digraphs *oo, ou, ew*

Spelling Words

soon
new
noon
zoo
boot
too
moon
blew
soup
you

Write each group of Spelling Words in ABC order.

soon	moon	too	new
noon	zoo	blew	soup
boot		you	
_____		_____	
_____		_____	
_____		_____	
_____		_____	
_____		_____	
_____		_____	
_____		_____	
_____		_____	
_____		_____	
_____		_____	
_____		_____	
_____		_____	
_____		_____	
_____		_____	

© Houghton Mifflin Harcourt Publishing Company. All rights reserved.

Name _____

Indefinite Pronouns

Indefinite pronouns stand for people or things that are not named.

Word Bank

anyone	someone	everyone
something	everybody	everything

Write an indefinite pronoun from the Word Bank to complete each sentence.

1. We met _____ in the park.
2. Did you bring _____ to eat.
3. Can _____ pick apples with me?
4. I put _____ in the box.
5. _____ likes red apples.

© Houghton Mifflin Harcourt Publishing Company. All rights reserved.

Name _____

A Tree Is a Plant
Spelling: Words with *oo, ou, ew*

Spelling Words with the *oo* (moon) Sound

Spelling Words

soon
new
noon
zoo
boot
too
moon
blew
soup
you

Write the Spelling Word that completes each sentence.

1. We will have our lunch at _____ _____ _____ _____ .
2. I hope that I will see you _____ _____ _____ _____ .
3. The wind _____ _____ _____ _____ the tree over.
4. I saw many animals at the _____ _____ _____ _____ .
5. There was a full _____ _____ _____ _____ last night.
6. It is _____ _____ _____ _____ hot to play outside.
7. We will have _____ _____ _____ _____ for lunch.
8. I need a _____ _____ _____ _____ pencil.

© Houghton Mifflin Harcourt Publishing Company. All rights reserved.

Name _____

Spiral Review

Rewrite each sentence to tell about the future.

1. It stopped raining.

2. I picked apples.

3. We learn about trees.

4. I climbed a tree.

5. They planted new trees.

© Houghton Mifflin Harcourt Publishing Company. All rights reserved.

Name _____

A Tree Is a Plant
Writing: Narrative Writing

Planning My Story

Write and draw details for your story.

Characters	Setting

Plot

Beginning

Middle

End

© Houghton Mifflin Harcourt Publishing Company. All rights reserved.

Name _____

Grammar in Writing

A Tree Is a Plant
Grammar: Indefinite Pronouns

Use **indefinite pronouns** to stand for the names of people or things. They do not name certain people or things.

Word Bank

anyone	**something**	**someone**
everything	**everyone**	**everybody**

Write an indefinite pronoun from the Word Bank to complete each sentence.

1. _____ went to the farm.
2. The farmer knew _____ about apples.
3. She helped _____ pick apples.
4. She didn't want _____ to get hurt.

© Houghton Mifflin Harcourt Publishing Company. All rights reserved.

Name _____

The New Friend
Phonics: Words with *ou, ow*

Words with *ou, ow*

Circle the word that names the picture.

1.

cot cow

2.

couch coach

3.

moose mouse

4.

crow crown

5.

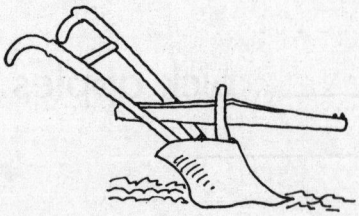

plate plow

6.

cloud closed

© Houghton Mifflin Harcourt Publishing Company. All rights reserved.

Name _____

Words to Know

The New Friend
High-Frequency Words

Draw a line to match each picture to the word that goes with it.

1. 

2. 

3. 

4. 

5. 

6. 

family

school

party

city

buy

myself

Use the words **seven** and **please** together in a sentence. Write it on the line.

_____

_____

_____

© Houghton Mifflin Harcourt Publishing Company. All rights reserved.

Name _____

The New Friend
Phonics: Words with *ou, ow*

Words with *ou, ow*

Circle the word that best completes each sentence.

1. I got a new pet. He's a _____ dog.

hound **hold**

2. He should not jump up on the _____.

coach **couch**

3. At night, my dog _____ at the moon.

holes **howls**

4. My dog's bark is very _____.

loud **load**

5. He will _____ when someone comes to the house!

grow **growl**

6. He sits when I tell him to get _____.

down **dome**

© Houghton Mifflin Harcourt Publishing Company. All rights reserved.

Name _____

The New Friend
Spelling: Words with *ow, ou*

Spelling Words with Vowel Diphthongs *ow*, *ou*

Sort the words. Write the correct Spelling Words in each column.

Words with ou	Words with ow

Spelling Words

how
now
cow
owl
ouch
house
found
out
gown
town

© Houghton Mifflin Harcourt Publishing Company. All rights reserved.

Name _____

The New Friend
Grammar: Contractions

Contractions with *not*

Write a contraction from the box for the underlined word or words.

Word Bank

isn't
aren't
can't
don't

1. This house is not empty now.

_____

_____

2. I do not know where my books are.

_____

_____

3. They are not in this big box.

_____

_____

4. I cannot find my jump rope.

_____

_____

5. I do not have a new friend yet.

_____

_____

© Houghton Mifflin Harcourt Publishing Company. All rights reserved.

Name _____

The New Friend
Writing: Narrative Writing

Sentences with Different Lengths

Make long sentences by joining two short sentences with and.

1. Kirk moved to a new city. He was happy.

_____

_____ ,

_____

and _____ .

2. The city is far away. It is very big.

_____

_____ ,

_____

and _____ .

3. Kirk made new friends. He saw new places.

_____

_____ ,

_____

and _____ .

© Houghton Mifflin Harcourt Publishing Company. All rights reserved.

Name _____

The New Friend
Phonics: Words with *oi, oy, au, aw*

Words with *oi, oy, au, aw*

Circle the two words in each row that have the same vowel sound. Write the letters that stand for the sound.

				oi	oy	au	aw
1.	coins	coats	join				
2.	joy	boy	book				
3.	house	sauce	pause				
4.	dune	dawn	crawl				
5.	point	paint	moist				

© Houghton Mifflin Harcourt Publishing Company. All rights reserved.

Name _____ Date _____

Reader's Guide

The New Friend

Meet Makoto!

You get to introduce Makoto to his classmates!

Read pages 166–173. Write three things you know about Makoto. Draw a picture of him.

© Houghton Mifflin Harcourt Publishing Company. All rights reserved.

Name _____ Date _____

The New Friend
Independent Reading

Read pages 174–181. Makoto wants to bring something to show the class more about his life. Draw a picture to show what he brings. Then write a sentence to tell why he chose it.

© Houghton Mifflin Harcourt Publishing Company. All rights reserved.

Name _____

The New Friend
Spelling: Words with *ou, ow*

Spelling Words with Vowel Diphthongs *ou*, *ow*

Spelling Words

how
now
cow
owl
ouch
house
found
out
gown
town

Write the Spelling Word that fits each clue.

1. Opposite of **later** _____

2. Opposite of **lost** _____

3. A farm animal _____

4. Smaller than a city _____

5. Opposite of **in** _____

6. A bird _____

© Houghton Mifflin Harcourt Publishing Company. All rights reserved.

Name _____

The New Friend
Grammar: Contractions

Contractions with Pronouns

Write a contraction from the box for the underlined words.

Word Bank

I'm he's she's it's

1. It is a pretty day.
_____
_____

2. I am going to school with my new friend.
_____
_____

3. He is in the car with his mom.
_____
_____

4. She is driving us.
_____
_____

© Houghton Mifflin Harcourt Publishing Company. All rights reserved.

Name _____

The New Friend
Spelling: Words with *ow* and *ou*

Spelling Words with *ow* and *ou*

Spelling Words

how
house
now
owl
cow
found
town
ouch
out
gown

Write the Spelling Word that completes each sentence.

1. We're walking to my _____.
2. _____ will you get home?
3. Do you live far from _____?
4. I'm going _____ to play.
5. _____! That hurt!
6. He's coming home right _____.

© Houghton Mifflin Harcourt Publishing Company. All rights reserved.

Name _____

The New Friend
Grammar

Spiral Review

Circle the prepositional phrase in each sentence. Decide if the prepositional phrase tells where or when. Write where or when on the line.

1. Max and Viv play after school. _____
2. They meet in the park. _____
3. Viv's kite is stuck in a tree. _____
4. They race on the grass. _____
5. The park closes at five o'clock. _____
6. The friends will meet again next week. _____

© Houghton Mifflin Harcourt Publishing Company. All rights reserved.

Name _____

Grammar in Writing

The New Friend
Grammar: Contractions

- A contraction is a short way of writing some words.
- This mark (') takes the place of missing letters.

Fix the mistakes in these sentences.
Use proofreading marks.

Example: ~~H'es~~ He's in a new house.

1. Im' with my new friend.

2. Today shes putting her toys away.

3. She cant' find the games.

4. The books are'nt in the box.

5. We do'nt play today.

Proofreading Marks	
^	add
⁓	take out

© Houghton Mifflin Harcourt Publishing Company. All rights reserved.

Name _____

The Dot
Phonics: Adding *-ed, -ing*

Adding *-ed*, *-ing*

Look at the picture. Read the word. Circle the -ed or -ing word that is spelled correctly.

1.	 hop	hoping hopeing hopping
2.	 bat	batted bated bateed
3.	 skate	skating skatting skateing
4.	 bike	bikked biked bikeed
5.	 hug	huging hugging hugiing
6.	 wave	waved waveed wavvd

© Houghton Mifflin Harcourt Publishing Company. All rights reserved.

Name _____

Words to Know

The Dot
High-Frequency Words

Circle the correct word to complete each sentence.

1. A (even, teacher) helps you learn.

2. Please push that box (toward, pushed) me.

3. A (bear, surprised) is a big animal.

4. The lamp is (above, pushed) the shelf.

5. Mom (teacher, pushed) Kim on the swing.

6. Jim was (surprised, even) by his birthday gift.

7. All the family came, (even, above) Grandma.

8. Ben (toward, studied) the painting closely.

© Houghton Mifflin Harcourt Publishing Company. All rights reserved.

Name _____

The Dot
Phonics: Adding *-ed, -ing*

Adding *-ed*, *-ing*

Circle the word that fits in the sentence.

1. The cowboy _____ a cow.

ropped **roped**

2. A clown was _____ a red flag.

waveing **waving**

3. The bull _____ running.

stoped **stopped**

4. Kate _____ Silver.

peted **petted**

© Houghton Mifflin Harcourt Publishing Company. All rights reserved.

Name _____

The Dot
Spelling: Words Ending in *-ed, -ing*

Spelling Words Ending in *-ed*, *-ing*

Spelling Words

mix
mixed
hop
hopped
hope
hoping
run
running
use
used

Write the Spelling Words that end in -ing.

1. _____ 2. _____

Write the Spelling Words that end in -ed.

3. _____ 4. _____

5. _____

Write the Spelling Words that are base words.

6. _____ 7. _____

8. _____ 9. _____

10. _____

© Houghton Mifflin Harcourt Publishing Company. All rights reserved.

Name _____

The Dot
Grammar: Exclamations

What Is an Exclamation?

Draw a line under each exclamation.

1. The art show was great!

I saw many paintings.

2. Did you see the painting of the dog?

I liked that one the most!

3. Dee and Jan put the show together.

They did a good job!

4. I hope our class can see that show!

Don't you think so, too?

5. Kay saw the show yesterday.

She wants to see it again!

© Houghton Mifflin Harcourt Publishing Company. All rights reserved.

The Dot
Writing: Opinion Writing

Name _____

Showing Strong Feelings

Finish these sentences that tell your opinion about Vashti's teacher. Write one exclamation that shows a strong feeling.

Topic Sentence

I think Vashti's teacher is _____

Detail Sentence

I think so because _____

Detail Sentence

I also think so because _____

© Houghton Mifflin Harcourt Publishing Company. All rights reserved.

Name _____

The Dot
Phonics: Long *e* Spelling Patterns *y, ie*

Words with Long *e* Spelling Patterns *y, ie*

Circle the word that matches the picture. Write the word.

1.

bus bunny

_____

_____

2.

park party

_____

_____

3.

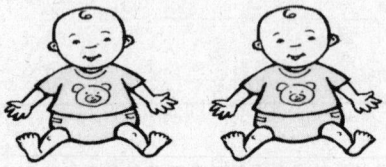

baby babies

_____

_____

4.

chief cheese

_____

_____

5.

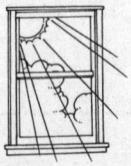

sunny seed

_____

_____

6.

when windy

_____

_____

© Houghton Mifflin Harcourt Publishing Company. All rights reserved.

Name _____ Date _____

Reader's Guide

The Dot

Art Awards

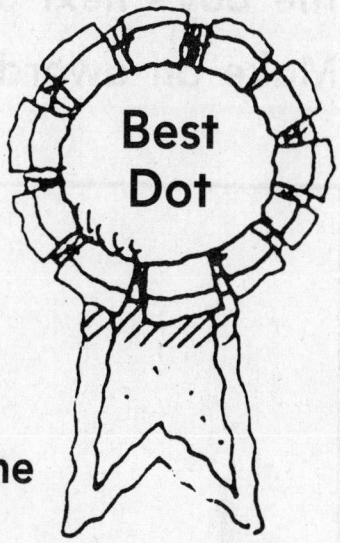

Art shows often have awards. The awards are given to the best pieces of art.

Read pages 15–29. Here is an award for the best artwork at the art show.

Which artwork won this award?

Why did it win the award?

© Houghton Mifflin Harcourt Publishing Company. All rights reserved.

Name _____ Date _____

The Dot
Independent Reading

Read pages 30–33. Draw what you think the boy's next artwork will look like. Make an award for it.

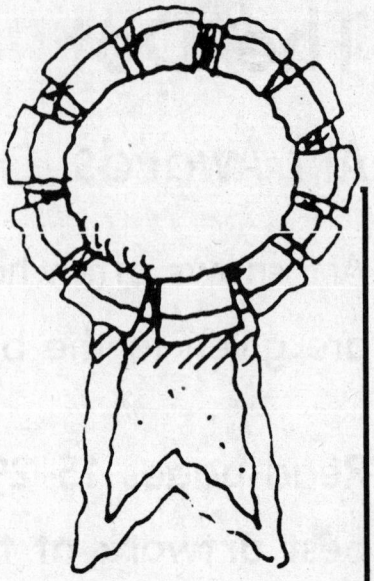

Why did it win this award?

_____

_____

_____

_____

_____

© Houghton Mifflin Harcourt Publishing Company. All rights reserved.

Name _____

The Dot
Spelling: Words Ending in *-ed, -ing*

Spelling Words Ending in *-ed*, *-ing*

Spelling Words

mix
mixed
hop
hopped
hope
hoping
run
running
use
used

Add -ed to each base word. Then write the new Spelling Word on the line.

1. mix _____

2. hop _____

3. use _____

Add -ing to each base word. Then write the new Spelling Word on the line.

4. hope _____

5. run _____

© Houghton Mifflin Harcourt Publishing Company. All rights reserved.

Name _____

Writing Exclamations

The Dot
Grammar: Exclamations

Write each sentence as an exclamation. Begin and end the sentences correctly.

1. those paints are pretty

2. i love these new pencils

3. this painting got a prize

4. there is too much paper

5. we can't wait to draw

© Houghton Mifflin Harcourt Publishing Company. All rights reserved.

Name _____

The Dot
Writing: Opinion Writing

Planning My Sentences

Write your opinion. Then write reasons that tell why. Include a closing sentence.

My Opinion

First Reason

Second Reason

Closing Sentence

© Houghton Mifflin Harcourt Publishing Company. All rights reserved.

Name _____

The Dot
Spelling: Words with *-ed* and *-ing*

Words with Endings *-ed* and *-ing*

Write the Spelling Word to complete each sentence.

_____

1. The bunny _____ away.
   (hop, hopped)
   _____

2. I _____ I will win the race.
   (hope, hoping)
   _____

3. He is _____ very fast.
   (run, running)
   _____

4. Kim _____ all the glue in her art project.
   (use, used)
   _____

5. I _____ the eggs and the butter.
   (mix, mixed)

© Houghton Mifflin Harcourt Publishing Company. All rights reserved.

Name _____

Spiral Review

Circle the pronoun that can take the place of the underlined word or words.

1. Jack and Fred want to paint.

   We **They** **He**

2. Roy drew a picture of a puppy.

   It **He** **She**

3. The picture is very big.

   We **It** **He**

Write He, She, It, We, or They to take the place of the underlined word or words.

4. Jenny went to the art store. _____

5. Rob and Liz were there. _____

6. The store is a fun place. _____

© Houghton Mifflin Harcourt Publishing Company. All rights reserved.

Name _____

Grammar in Writing

The Dot
Grammar: Exclamations

An **exclamation** is a sentence that shows strong feeling. It ends with an exclamation point (!).

Example: Meg is an artist.

Revised: Meg is the best artist I know!

Revise each sentence. Make it an exclamation.

1. I like blue.

_____

_____

2. Mandy drew a picture.

_____

_____

3. Karl likes to paint.

_____

_____

4. Your pictures are nice.

_____

_____

© Houghton Mifflin Harcourt Publishing Company. All rights reserved.

Name _____

What Can You Do?
Phonics: Adding *-er, -est* (change *y* to *i*)

Adding *-er*, *-est* (change *y* to *i*)

Read the words. Circle the word that does not belong.

1. fancy	fancier	fanciest	find
2. happy	happier	hand	happiest
3. silly	sillier	silliest	still
4. funny	far	funnier	funniest
5. jolly	jollier	jolliest	joke
6. messy	miss	messier	messiest

© Houghton Mifflin Harcourt Publishing Company. All rights reserved.

Name _____

Words to Know

What Can You Do?
High-Frequency Words

Circle the best answer to each question.

1. What word goes with **far**? **near** **high**
2. What word goes with **plot**? **always** **stories**
3. What word goes with **when**? **different** **once**
4. What word goes with **just right**? **enough** **near**
5. What word goes with **low**? **high** **happy**
6. What word goes with **sad**? **once** **happy**
7. What word goes with **never**? **high** **always**
8. What word goes with **same**? **different** **stories**

© Houghton Mifflin Harcourt Publishing Company. All rights reserved.

Name _____

What Can You Do?
Phonics: Adding *-er*, *-est* (change *y* to *i*)

Adding *-er*, *-est* (change *y* to *i*)

Circle the word that best completes the sentence.

1. My glue is _____ .

sticky **stickier**

2. That chick is the _____ of all.

fluffy **fluffiest**

3. This cupcake is _____ .

yummy **yummiest**

4. My hat is the _____ of all.

fancier **fanciest**

5. Her bird makes the _____ sounds.

sillier **silliest**

6. Luke tells _____ jokes.

funny **funnier**

© Houghton Mifflin Harcourt Publishing Company. All rights reserved.

Name _____

What Can You Do?
Spelling: Words Ending in *-er, -est*

Spelling Words Ending in *-er*, *-est*

Spelling Words

hard
harder
hardest
fast
faster
fastest
slow
slower
slowest
sooner

Sort the words. Write the correct Spelling Words in each column.

Words with -er	Words with -est
_____	_____
_____	_____
_____	_____
_____	_____
_____	_____
_____	_____
_____	_____
_____	_____
_____	_____
_____	_____
_____	_____
_____	_____

Base Words

_____	_____	_____
_____	_____	_____
_____	_____	_____

© Houghton Mifflin Harcourt Publishing Company. All rights reserved.

Name _____

What Can You Do?
Grammar: Kinds of Sentences

Question, Exclamation, Statement, or Command?

Draw a line from each question to the question mark (?). Draw a line from each exclamation to the exclamation point (!). Draw a line from each statement or command to the period(.).

1. I really love to sing

?

!

2. Do you play drums

?

!

3. Give the children a snack

?

.

4. Mark makes the snacks

?

.

5. May I have one

?

.

© Houghton Mifflin Harcourt Publishing Company. All rights reserved.

Name _____

What Can You Do?
Writing: Opinion Writing

Write Sentences with *Because*

Finish these sentences that tell your opinion about learning something new.

Topic Sentence

_____ _____

Learning to _____ is _____ .
hard easy

Detail Sentence _____

One reason is _____ .

Detail Sentence _____

Another reason is _____ .

Closing Sentence

_____ _____

Learning to _____ is _____ .

© Houghton Mifflin Harcourt Publishing Company. All rights reserved.

Name _____

Syllable *-le*

What Can You Do?
Phonics: Syllable *-le*

Circle the word that names the picture.

1.

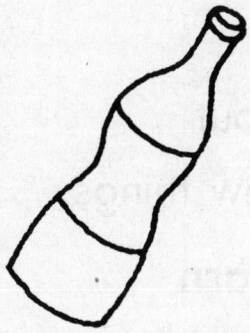

bottle bubble

2.

handle candle

3.

paddle apple

4.

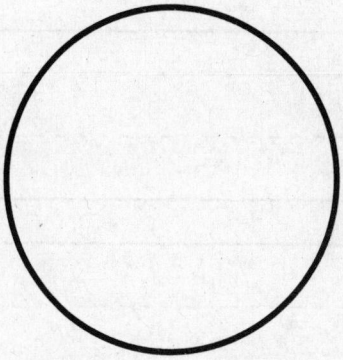

circle cattle

5.

bumble beetle

6.

poodle puzzle

© Houghton Mifflin Harcourt Publishing Company. All rights reserved.

Name _____ Date _____

What Can You Do?

Lessons to Learn

The selection has important lessons about practicing, trying hard, and learning new things.

Read pages 51–59. What did you learn about practicing?

_____

_____

_____

_____

_____

_____

_____

_____

_____

_____

Read pages 60–69. What is the moral or lesson of the whole selection?

_____

_____

_____

_____

_____

© Houghton Mifflin Harcourt Publishing Company. All rights reserved.

Name _____ Date _____

What Can You Do?
Independent Reading

Think of two animal characters who have a problem they can fix by practicing. List the characters and the setting. Tell what happens first, next, and last. Then write your story on another sheet of paper.

My Characters	My Setting

Events in My Story

© Houghton Mifflin Harcourt Publishing Company. All rights reserved.

Name _____

What Can You Do?
Spelling: Words ending in *-er, -est*

Spelling Words Ending in *-er*, *-est*

Spelling Words

hard
harder
hardest
fast
faster
fastest
slow
slower
slowest
sooner

Add **-er** to each base word. Then write the new Spelling Word on the line.

1. hard _____
2. fast _____
3. slow _____
4. soon _____

Add **-est** to each base word. Then write the Spelling Word on the line.

5. hard _____
6. fast _____
7. slow _____

© Houghton Mifflin Harcourt Publishing Company. All rights reserved.

Name _____

Kinds of Sentences

What Can You Do?
Grammar: Kinds of Sentences

Combine the two shorter sentences to write a compound sentence.

1. Go home. Come with us.

, or

2. Dan loves to run! He loves to swim even more!

, but

3. I can knit. I can sew.

, and

4. Will Jen come home soon? Will she be out late?

, or

© Houghton Mifflin Harcourt Publishing Company. All rights reserved.

Name _____

Planning My Sentences

What Can You Do?
Writing: Opinion Writing

Write your opinion. Then write reasons that tell why.

My Opinion

First Reason

Second Reason

Closing Sentence

© Houghton Mifflin Harcourt Publishing Company. All rights reserved.

Name _____

What Can You Do?
Spelling: Words with *-er* and *-est*

Words with Endings *-er* and *-est*

Write the Spelling Word that completes each sentence.

fast **faster** **fastest**

1. The bus goes _____ .
2. The truck goes _____ than the bus.
3. The car goes the _____ .

slow **slower** **slowest**

4. The bug is _____ .
5. The worm is _____ than the bug.
6. The turtle is the _____ of all.

© Houghton Mifflin Harcourt Publishing Company. All rights reserved.

Name _____

Spiral Review

What Can You Do?
Grammar

Choose the correct words from the word box to finish each sentence.

Mark	I	me

_____ _____

1. _____ and _____ act in a play.

I	Tammy	me

_____ _____

2. The teacher reads _____ and _____ a story.

me	I	Ricky

_____ _____

3. Nana watches _____ and _____ .

I	me	Sue

_____ _____

4. _____ and _____ like to slide.

© Houghton Mifflin Harcourt Publishing Company. All rights reserved.

Name _____

Grammar in Writing

What Can You Do?
Grammar: Kinds of Sentences

A **statement** and a **command** end with a period. A **question** ends with a question mark. An **exclamation** ends with an exclamation point. All sentences begin with capital letters.

Revise each sentence. Change it to the kind shown in ( ).

Example: Glen can read. (question)
Can Glen read?

1. Is skating fun? (statement)

_____

2. I like to ride my bike. (exclamation)

_____

3. Chuck likes to act. (question)

_____

4. You write a story. (command)

_____

© Houghton Mifflin Harcourt Publishing Company. All rights reserved.

Name _____

The Kite
Phonics: Long *i* Spelling Patterns *igh, y, ie*

Long *i* Spelling Patterns *igh*, *y*, *ie*

Look at the picture. Circle the word that names the picture.

1. 

spy line

2. 

pine pie

3. 

sky nine

4. 

high hive

5. 

think thigh

6. 

fine fly

© Houghton Mifflin Harcourt Publishing Company. All rights reserved.

Name _____

Words to Know

The Kite
High-Frequency Words

Circle the correct word in each sentence.

1. The cat plays with a (ball, head) of yarn.

2. We all (cried, heard) the crash.

3. You (heard, should) try these grapes.

4. Jean is the (second, ball) girl in line.

5. "Let's go!" (cried, heard) Kenny.

6. My (large, head) hurts.

7. We are running (second, across) the field.

8. There is a (large, heard) bird in the tree.

© Houghton Mifflin Harcourt Publishing Company. All rights reserved.

Name _____

The Kite
Phonics: Long *i* Spelling Patterns *igh, y, ie*

Long *i* Spelling Patterns *igh*, *y*, *ie*

Write a word from the box to finish each sentence.

thigh	dry	try	tie	high

1. Sam hurt his _____ when he fell.

2. Dad's _____ has dots and stripes.

3. I will _____ to swim.

4. The bird will fly up _____.

5. The wet shirt will _____.

© Houghton Mifflin Harcourt Publishing Company. All rights reserved.

The Kite
Spelling: Words with Patterns *igh, y, ie*

Name _____

Spelling Words with Patterns *igh*, *y*, *ie*

Spelling Words

my
try
sky
fly
by
dry
pie
cried
night
light

Write the Spelling Words with the igh pattern.

1. _____ 2. _____

Write the Spelling Words with the ie pattern.

3. _____ 4. _____

Write the Spelling Words with the y spelling.

5. _____ 6. _____

7. _____ 8. _____

9. _____ 10. _____

© Houghton Mifflin Harcourt Publishing Company. All rights reserved.

Name _____

The Kite
Grammar: Kinds of Adjectives

Adjectives for Taste and Smell

Draw a line under each adjective. Then write the adjective.

1. I smell the sweet roses.

_____

2. We taste the bitter lemon.

_____

3. Does the milk smell sour?

_____

Draw a line under each adjective and add commas where they are needed.

4. Some nuts are crunchy sweet and salty.

5. The fruit was sweet moist and chewy.

© Houghton Mifflin Harcourt Publishing Company. All rights reserved.

Name _____

Using Different Words

The Kite
Writing: Opinion Writing

Change a repeated word to an exact word. Use a word from the box or your own.

bright	down	high
flew	funny	blue
mean	ran	sunny

Toad <u>went</u> fast, and the kite <u>went</u> up.

_____

Toad _____ fast, and the kite went up.

The <u>little</u> birds laughed at Toad's <u>little</u> kite.

_____

The little birds laughed at Toad's _____ kite.

The <u>pretty</u> kite danced in the <u>pretty</u> sky.

_____

The pretty kite danced in the _____ sky.

© Houghton Mifflin Harcourt Publishing Company. All rights reserved.

Name _____

The Kite
Phonics: Adding *-ed, -ing, -er, -est, -es*

Adding *-ed, -ing, -er, -est, -es*

Write the word that best completes each sentence. Use words from the box.

smaller	jumped	riding	highest	foxes

1. Those trees are the _____ of all.

2. That bird is _____ than this one.

3. Who is _____ a red bike?

4. A frog _____ into the pond.

5. Five _____ ran to the woods.

© Houghton Mifflin Harcourt Publishing Company. All rights reserved.

Name _____ Date _____

Reader's Guide

The Kite

Frog, Toad, and the Robins

Read pages 88–93. The robins made fun of the kite. Now draw a cartoon. Draw Frog. Make a speech bubble to show what he says to the robins.

© Houghton Mifflin Harcourt Publishing Company. All rights reserved.

Name _____ Date _____

The Kite
Independent Reading

Read pages 94–101. Now draw a cartoon. Show what Frog might say to the robins at the end of the story.

© Houghton Mifflin Harcourt Publishing Company. All rights reserved.

The Kite
Spelling: Words with Patterns *igh, y, ie*

Name _____

Spelling Words with Patterns *igh*, *y*, *ie*

Spelling Words

my
try
sky
fly
by
dry
pie
cried
night
light

Write each group of Spelling Words in ABC order.

my	try	dry	pie
sky	fly	cried	night
by		light	

© Houghton Mifflin Harcourt Publishing Company. All rights reserved.

Name _____

The Kite
Grammar: Adjectives

Adjectives for Sound and Texture

Draw a line under each adjective. Then write the adjective.

1. We sail on the smooth lake.

_____

2. I hear the loud cry of a seagull.

_____

3. The blanket feels warm.

_____

Draw a line under each adjective and add commas where they are needed.

4. The beat was noisy loud and pounding.

5. The music was soft catchy and nice.

© Houghton Mifflin Harcourt Publishing Company. All rights reserved.

Name _____

Planning My Sentences

The Kite
Writing: Opinion Writing

Write your opinion. Then write reasons that tell why. Include a closing sentence.

My Opinion

First Reason

Second Reason

Closing Sentence

© Houghton Mifflin Harcourt Publishing Company. All rights reserved.

Name _____

The Kite
Spelling: Words with *igh, y, ie*

Spelling Words with *igh, y, ie*

Write the correct word to complete each sentence.

1. Please turn on the _____.
   (cried, light, pie)

2. Have you seen _____ book?
   (my, try, night)

3. The baby _____ in her crib.
   (fly, dry, cried)

4. Make sure to _____ the dishes.
   (dry, my, light)

5. We went to a great play last _____.
   (light, night, fly)

© Houghton Mifflin Harcourt Publishing Company. All rights reserved.

Name _____

Spiral Review

Write the correct pronoun to finish each sentence.

1. Is the yellow kite _____ ?

   your **yours**

2. That is _____ kite.

   her **hers**

3. Rex put away _____ kite.

   he **his**

4. Would you like to play at _____ house?

   my **mine**

5. We went to _____ party.

   their **theirs**

© Houghton Mifflin Harcourt Publishing Company. All rights reserved.

Name _____

The Kite
Grammar: Kinds of Adjectives

Grammar in Writing

Some adjectives describe nouns by telling about **taste**, **smell**, **sound**, or **feel**.

Example: I feel the cool breeze.
^

Revise each sentence. Use the proofreading mark to add an adjective.

sweet	fresh	happy	soft

1. Mr. Bee shares some honey.

2. The frog gave a croak.

3. We sit on the grass.

4. We enjoy the air.

Proofreading Mark	
^	add

© Houghton Mifflin Harcourt Publishing Company. All rights reserved.

Name _____

Hi! Fly Guy
Phonics: Words with Suffixes *-ful, -ly, -y*

Suffixes *-ful*, *-ly*, *-y*

Write a suffix from the box to finish the word.

ful	ly	y

1.

_____

sad _____

2.

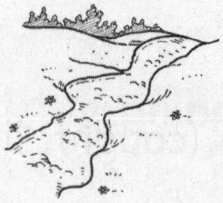

_____

bump _____

3.

_____

dust _____

4.

_____

help _____

5.

_____

slow _____

6.

_____

safe _____

© Houghton Mifflin Harcourt Publishing Company. All rights reserved.

Name _____

Words to Know

Circle the correct word to complete each sentence.

1. Planting vegetables is a good (minute, idea).

2. Juan (caught, listen) the ball.

3. Mom (took, caught) us for a haircut.

4. Nancy (idea, thought) about what to bake.

5. My sister has a (beautiful, friendship) new bike.

6. Please (listen, took) to the teacher.

7. My cousin will be here in a (minute, listen).

8. My (beautiful, friendship) with Rita is important to me.

© Houghton Mifflin Harcourt Publishing Company. All rights reserved.

Name _____

Hi! Fly Guy
Phonics: Words with Suffixes *-ful, -ly, -y*

Suffixes *-ful*, *-ly*, *-y*

Choose a word from the box. Choose a suffix to make a new word. Write the new word below the suffix.

spoon	snow	sad	trick	
joy	quick	peace	dirt	glad

y	ly	ful
_____	_____	_____
_____	_____	_____
_____	_____	_____
_____	_____	_____
_____	_____	_____
_____	_____	_____
_____	_____	_____
_____	_____	_____

© Houghton Mifflin Harcourt Publishing Company. All rights reserved.

Name _____

Hi! Fly Guy
Spellling: Words with *-ly, -y, -ful*

Spelling Words with the Suffixes *-ly, -y, -ful*

Spelling Words

sad
sadly
slow
slowly
dust
dusty
trick
tricky
help
helpful

Write the Spelling Words with -ly.

1. _____ 2. _____

Write the Spelling Words with -y.

3. _____ 4. _____

Write the Spelling Word with -ful.

5. _____

Write the Spelling Words that are base words.

6. _____ 7. _____

8. _____ 9. _____

10. _____

© Houghton Mifflin Harcourt Publishing Company. All rights reserved.

Name _____

Hi! Fly Guy
Grammar: Adverbs

Adverbs for How and Where

Circle the adverb in each sentence. Write it on the line.

1. The man went upstairs. _____
2. The dog followed him closely. _____
3. Buzz is here. _____
4. He watched the fly carefully. _____

Complete each sentence. Write an adverb that tells how or where.

5. The leaf floated _____ down the stream.
6. Jose stores his new boat _____.

© Houghton Mifflin Harcourt Publishing Company. All rights reserved.

Name _____

Hi! Fly Guy
Writing: Opinion Writing

Giving Examples

Look at the picture of the judges on page 139 of your book. Write your opinion about how the judges are feeling about their decision.

I think the judges are feeling _____.

Write one reason to explain your opinion.

One reason is _____

Write two examples to explain your reason.

1. _____

2. _____

© Houghton Mifflin Harcourt Publishing Company. All rights reserved.

Hi! Fly Guy
Phonics: Long Vowel Spelling Patterns: *a, e, i, o, u*

Name _____

Long Vowel Spelling Patterns *a, e, i, o, u*

Circle the two words in each row that rhyme. Then write the letter that spells the long vowel sound.

1.

table hi fable me _____ _____

2.

hi she he go _____ _____

3.

kind no flu mind _____ _____

4.

flu Stu so be _____ _____

5.

we hold wind told _____ _____

© Houghton Mifflin Harcourt Publishing Company. All rights reserved.

Name _____ Date _____

Reader's Guide

Hi! Fly Guy

Fly Talk

You have a special machine.

It tells you what Fly says!

Read pages 119–125. Use your imagination! What does Fly Guy mean when he says "Buzz!" on page 124?

Read pages 126–128. What does Fly Guy mean when he says "Buzz!" on page 128?

© Houghton Mifflin Harcourt Publishing Company. All rights reserved.

Name _____ Date _____

Hi! Fly Guy
Independent Reading

Read pages 129–130. What does Fly Guy mean when he says "Buzz!" on page 130?

Read pages 131–141. What does Fly Guy mean when he says "Buzz!" on page 136?

© Houghton Mifflin Harcourt Publishing Company. All rights reserved.

Name _____

Hi! Fly Guy
Spelling: Words with *-ly, -y, -ful*

Spelling Words with the Suffixes *-ly, -y, -ful*

Spelling Words

sad
sadly
slow
slowly
dust
dusty
trick
tricky
help
helpful

Add -ly to each base word. Then write the new Spelling Word on the line.

1. sad _____

2. slow _____

Add -y to each base word. Then write the new Spelling Word on the line.

3. dust _____

4. trick _____

Add -ful to the base word. Then write the new Spelling Word on the line.

5. help _____

© Houghton Mifflin Harcourt Publishing Company. All rights reserved.

Name _____

Hi! Fly Guy
Grammar: Adverbs

Adverbs for When and How Much

Circle the adverb in each sentence. Write it on the line.

1. The wagon is too heavy to pull. _____

2. Dwayne arrived late to the picnic. _____

3. He was very happy to see his friends. _____

4. They will have a ball game soon. _____

Complete each sentence. Write an adverb that tells when or how much.

5. We will have a pet show _____.

6. The bucket was _____ full.

© Houghton Mifflin Harcourt Publishing Company. All rights reserved.

Name _____

Hi! Fly Guy
Spelling: Words with *-ly, -y, -ful*

Words with the Suffixes *-ly, -y, -ful*

Write the correct word from the box to complete each sentence.

1. I did a card _____.

trick
tricky

2. It was _____ to find the way to the park.

trick
tricky

3. I like to _____ wash the car.

help
helpful

4. When I wash the car, I am very _____.

help
helpful

5. I was _____ to hear my mom call me home.

sad
sadly

6. I _____ walked home.

sad
sadly

© Houghton Mifflin Harcourt Publishing Company. All rights reserved.

Name _____

Spiral Review

Indefinite pronouns stand for the names of people or things. They do not take the place of a noun for a certain person or thing, though.

Write the indefinite pronoun that best completes the sentence.

1. Fly Guy knew _____ about being a pet.

something anyone

2. Buzz liked _____ about Fly Guy.

everyone everything

3. _____ was amazed by Fly Guy.

Everyone Everything

4. Did _____ teach Fly Guy his tricks?

everything someone

© Houghton Mifflin Harcourt Publishing Company. All rights reserved.

Name _____

Hi! Fly Guy
Writing: Opinion Writing

Planning My Opinion Paragraph

Write your opinion. Write reasons and examples. Then write a closing sentence.

My Opinion

First Reason

Example

Second Reason

Example

Closing Sentence

© Houghton Mifflin Harcourt Publishing Company. All rights reserved.

Name _____

Grammar in Writing

Hi! Fly Guy
Grammar: Adverbs

Adverbs can tell **how**, **where**, **when**, or **how much**.

Examples:	Buzz ran quickly.	how
	Buzz ran here.	where
	Buzz ran yesterday.	when
	Buzz ran a lot.	how much

Rewrite each sentence. Add the kind of adverb shown in ( ).

1. Flies find food. (where)

_____

_____

2. Fly Guy chewed a leaf. (when)

_____

_____

3. He chewed. (how)

_____

_____

4. He ate. (how much)

_____

_____

© Houghton Mifflin Harcourt Publishing Company. All rights reserved.

Name _____

Winners Never Quit!
Phonics: Syllabication (CV)

Syllable Pattern CV

Read each word. Draw a line to divide the CV word into two syllables.

1.

music might

2.

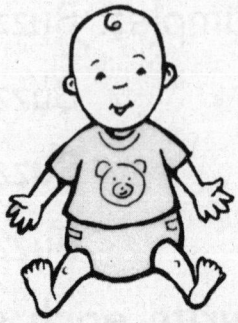

baby bone

3.

lace lady

4.

part pilot

5.

robber robot

6.

motel miss

© Houghton Mifflin Harcourt Publishing Company. All rights reserved.

Name _____

Words to Know

Winners Never Quit!
High-Frequency Words

Circle the best answer to each clue.

1. This means **all people.**	**everyone**	**field**
2. This means **liked a lot.**	**most**	**loved**
3. These are children and adults.	**sorry**	**people**
4. Sisters is its opposite.	**brothers**	**loved**
5. This is a place to play soccer.	**most**	**field**
6. This means **almost all.**	**people**	**most**
7. This means **a certain number.**	**field**	**only**
8. This is **a kind of feeling.**	**sorry**	**everyone**

© Houghton Mifflin Harcourt Publishing Company. All rights reserved.

Name _____

Winners Never Quit!
Phonics: Syllabication (CV)

Syllable Pattern CV

In each sentence, circle the CV word that has two syllables.

1. It is a bright, shiny day!

2. There is a huge hotel by the lake.

3. Big boats sail in the wavy tide.

4. I hope you decide to come see me.

5. We could take a slow, lazy ride on a boat.

© Houghton Mifflin Harcourt Publishing Company. All rights reserved.

Name _____

Winners Never Quit!
Spelling: Words with CV Syllables

Spelling Words with CV Syllables

Spelling Words

even
open
begin
baby
tiger
music
paper
zero
table
below

Write the Spelling Words with the long **e** sound in the first syllable.

1. _____
2. _____
3. _____
4. _____

Write the Spelling Words with the long **a** sound in the first syllable.

5. _____
6. _____
7. _____

Write the Spelling Words with these long vowel sounds in the first syllable.

8. long **i** _____
9. long **o** _____
10. long **u** _____

© Houghton Mifflin Harcourt Publishing Company. All rights reserved.

Name _____

Winners Never Quit!
Grammar: Adjectives That Compare

Adjectives with *er* and *est*

Circle the correct adjective to finish each sentence. Write the adjective.

1. Tim is _____ than Max.

taller **tallest**

_____

2. Fred is the _____ of them all.

taller **tallest**

_____

3. Cathy is _____ than Cam.

older **oldest**

_____

4. Adam is the _____ player of all.

smaller **smallest**

© Houghton Mifflin Harcourt Publishing Company. All rights reserved.

Name _____

Winners Never Quit!
Writing: Opinion Writing

Writing a Closing Sentence

Do you think Mia should have quit? Write your own words that explain your opinion. Listen to the words in the Word Bank. Read along. Be sure your last sentence retells your opinion.

Word Bank

agree disagree decision reason example

_____

I _____ with Mia's decision to

_____

quit. One reason is _____.

_____

For example, _____.

_____

Another reason is _____.

_____

I think _____.

© Houghton Mifflin Harcourt Publishing Company. All rights reserved.

Name _____

Winners Never Quit!
Phonics: Words with Prefixes *un-*, *re-*

Prefixes *un-*, *re-*

Read each word. Circle the word in each box that matches the picture.

1.

untie tried

2.

read repaint

3.

setting remove

4.

bedding unbraid

5.

untidy neat

6.

unzip unbutton

© Houghton Mifflin Harcourt Publishing Company. All rights reserved.

Name _____ Date _____

Reader's Guide

Winners Never Quit!

Soccer Stories

You just read about Mia Hamm, a famous soccer player. How do you think her brother and sister would tell the story?

Read pages 159–167. How do you think Lovdy would tell this part of the story?

© Houghton Mifflin Harcourt Publishing Company. All rights reserved.

Name _____ Date _____

Winners Never Quit!
Independent Reading

Read pages 168–177. How do you think Garrett would tell this part of the story?

Do you think Mia scored at the end? What do you think Lovdy and Garrett said to her?

© Houghton Mifflin Harcourt Publishing Company. All rights reserved.

Name _____

Winners Never Quit!
Spelling: Words with CV Syllables

Spelling Words with CV Syllables

Write the Spelling Word that fits each clue.

1. Opposite of **closed** _____

2. A very young person _____

3. Something to listen to _____

4. Opposite of **end** _____

5. Opposite of **above** _____

6. An animal _____

Spelling Words

even
open
begin
baby
tiger
music
paper
zero
table
below

© Houghton Mifflin Harcourt Publishing Company. All rights reserved.

Name _____

Winners Never Quit!
Grammar: Adjectives That Compare

Using the Right Adjective

Write adjectives from the Word Banks to finish the sentences.

Word Bank

green greener greenest

1. Our yard is _____ .
2. Your yard is _____ than ours.
3. His yard is the _____ of all.

Word Bank

long longer longest

4. We played a _____ game today.
5. The game yesterday was _____ than the game today.

© Houghton Mifflin Harcourt Publishing Company. All rights reserved.

Name _____

Winners Never Quit!
Spelling: Words with Syllable Pattern CV

Spelling Words with Syllable Pattern CV

Write the correct word to complete each sentence.

1. Ken saw a _____ at the zoo.
   (below, tiger)

2. Please sit and _____ your test.
   (even, begin)

3. What kind of _____ do you like?
   (below, music)

4. I used red _____ to make the card.
   (paper, zero)

5. The food is on the _____.
   (open, table)

© Houghton Mifflin Harcourt Publishing Company. All rights reserved.

Name _____

Spiral Review

Choose contractions from the box for the underlined words. Write the contractions.

Word Bank

He's
I'm
can't
They're
isn't

1. They are tennis players.
_____

2. I cannot wait to play with her.
_____

3. It is not hard to play.
_____

4. He is learning now!
_____

5. I am having fun.
_____

© Houghton Mifflin Harcourt Publishing Company. All rights reserved.

Name _____

Grammar in Writing

Winners Never Quit!
Grammar: Adjectives That Compare

- Add **er** to adjectives to compare two.
- Add **est** to compare more than two.

Example: Today is warm.

Today is the warmest day of the summer.

Revise each sentence. Use an adjective that compares. Add other words, too.

1. Beth is a fast runner.

_____

_____

2. Tad is tall.

_____

_____

3. Our team is stronger.

_____

_____

4. Today was cold.

_____

_____

© Houghton Mifflin Harcourt Publishing Company. All rights reserved.

Name _____ Date _____

Reader's Guide

Owl at Home

Case of the Messy Houseguest

Read pages 5–17. Owl thinks Winter came into his house and made a big mess. Is he right?

Write in the detective journal. What do you think really happened? Use clues from the text and pictures to explain your answer.

© Houghton Mifflin Harcourt Publishing Company. All rights reserved.

Name _____ Date _____

Owl at Home
Segment 1
Independent Reading

Case of the Mysterious Bumps

Read pages 19–29. There are two bumps at the bottom of Owl's bed. What are they?

Use your detective skills to solve the mystery! Write what you think the bumps are. Use clues from the text and pictures to explain your answer.

© Houghton Mifflin Harcourt Publishing Company. All rights reserved.

Name _____ Date _____

Reader's Guide

Owl at Home

Case of the Tear-Water Tea

Read pages 31–39. Owl makes salty tea. Why is the tea salty?

Write in the detective journal. Tell why the tea is salty. Use clues from the text and pictures to explain your answer.

© Houghton Mifflin Harcourt Publishing Company. All rights reserved.

Name _____ Date _____

Owl at Home
Segment 2
Independent Reading

Case of the Upstairs and Downstairs

Read pages 41–49. Help Owl understand why he cannot be upstairs and downstairs at the same time.

Use clues from the story to explain. Draw a picture and label it to solve the mystery for Owl.

© Houghton Mifflin Harcourt Publishing Company. All rights reserved.

Name _____ Date _____

Reader's Guide

Owl at Home

Case of the Moon Friend

Read pages 51–64. Owl looks at the moon and thinks it is a friend. Can the moon be Owl's friend?

Write your answer. Use clues from the text and pictures to explain.

© Houghton Mifflin Harcourt Publishing Company. All rights reserved.

Name _____ Date _____

Meet Owl

Use what you know about Owl to help him build a webpage. First, draw a picture of Owl in the box. Then fill in the blanks.

My Name: _____

I live in _____.

My favorite place is _____.

My favorite drink is _____.

My favorite thing to do is _____.

Right now, you can find me _____.

© Houghton Mifflin Harcourt Publishing Company. All rights reserved.